The Young Autistic Adult's Independence Handbook

The Young
AUTISTIC
ADULT'S
Independence
HANDBOOK

Haley Moss

Jessica Kingsley Publishers
London and Philadelphia

First published in Great Britain in 2022 by Jessica Kingsley Publishers
An Hachette Company

1

Copyright © Haley Moss 2022

Front cover image source: Shutterstock®

A CIP catalogue record for this title is available from the
British Library and the Library of Congress

ISBN 978 1 78775 757 8
eISBN 978 1 78775 758 5

Printed and bound in the United States by Integrated Books International

Jessica Kingsley Publishers' policy is to use papers that are natural,
renewable and recyclable products and made from wood grown in
sustainable forests. The logging and manufacturing processes are expected
to conform to the environmental regulations of the country of origin.

Jessica Kingsley Publishers
Carmelite House
50 Victoria Embankment
London EC4Y 0DZ

www.jkp.com

Contents

Acknowledgments

I have so many people to thank for their love, input, support, and positivity before and throughout this process.

Without my family, nothing would be possible, and I do not know where I would be. Thank you to my parents, Rick and Sherry Moss, for all you do each day for me and for our family. I love you so much, and writing this, like anything else I write, is a testament to you. Thank you for always believing in me. You cheered me on every single day without fail and I hope you recognize how much of your love went into this book. Thank you to my Aunt Sandy and Uncle Sam, Aunt Cathy and Uncle Scott, my grandfather Howard, and my other Aunt Sandy, for their unwavering love and support.

I must also thank the many folks who responded to my questions or agreed to speak with me for interviews and helped give me some expert perspectives. My knowledge is not fully complete, and I learned so much from each of you. Thank you to Doug Blecher, Dr Elizabeth Shea, Karla Helbert, and to so many others for your ideas, time, expertise, and support.

And, of course, my eternal thanks and gratitude to you, the reader, for sticking with me and for taking the time to read my thoughts and advice. You are ready for the world; the world better be ready for you.

Note from the Author

Adulthood is a time of transition where we grow as people, discover new things about ourselves, establish new habits and routines, and begin creating the lives we want to live. There are little transitions we make every day, like waking up and getting out of bed to eating breakfast, getting dressed, and heading off to work or school. There are also big transitions we make in life as young adults, like perhaps getting an apartment for the first time, graduating from school, and getting a new job. These transitions can be especially overwhelming to deal with as a young autistic adult. As young autistic people, we might be used to having others constantly guiding us and planning our lives, or be so set in our ways from being high school students or afraid of change, that any change of routine or plan can be enough to send us straight into meltdown city because of the uncertainty it brings.

There is also the hope many young autistic adults feel with the promise of independence and the chance to chase their own dreams, on their own terms. The world is full of infinite possibilities for young adults embarking on their journeys of self-discovery and independence. Autistic young adults deserve and are entitled to the same opportunities to find themselves and create lives for themselves where they feel valued, experience joy, and are able to be their authentic selves without feeling afraid. When I first moved four hours away from home for college, I remember the excitement over having new experiences like possibly finding new friends, exploring a new town, and learning what I wanted to do with my life when I "grew up" and graduated—all compounded with the nervousness of leaving home, possibly feeling homesick, or not knowing how to do "adult" things like actually take care of myself without my parents nagging me to dry my hair or eat three meals a day.

This book can hopefully make some parts of that journey through adulthood easier, or at least serve as a roadmap. We're often thrust into autistic adulthood with little expectation of how to manage our neurodivergent identity—we're told there is a very specific, neurotypical lens that we must follow to be successfully independent, responsible, dependable, well-adjusted, healthy, social, and law-abiding. However, there is no one specific way to be any of those things, and society does not often consider the way autistic people move throughout the world.

This book aims to empower young autistic people and give a little bit of guidance to not just surviving the adult world, but also doing it in a way that validates and affirms their authentic autistic selves, along with some advice from "more adult" autistic and allied neurotypical experts alike to add a little bit of knowledge into the toolbox for a successful transition to adulthood and young adult life.

What is "Independence" Anyway?

When I was 18 years old and getting ready to go off to college at the University of Florida, the idea of being independent sounded like a huge responsibility and an exciting journey to embark on. As someone who can count on one hand how many sleepovers they have had at friends' houses, and who never went to sleepaway (holiday) camp or stayed overnight with relatives, moving out and living in a tiny on-campus dorm room with another student was clearly supposed to feel like it would be the top of Independence Mountain.

It wasn't. I felt somewhat lost, actually.

I did not know every single "independent living skill," and those I did know I had not yet fully learned. I did not know anything about the workplace or money management at the time. My family spent most of the summer before college teaching me a crash course in living on my own—so I learned how to do a lot of household chores, and we packed and planned what stuff I would need to take to college with me.

The first day after my parents helped me move into my dorm room, everyone cried. I cried after I realized I was actually supposed to be on my own and living with a roommate. My parents cried driving the four hours back home without their newly adult college student child. I was not, all of a sudden, this magical adult figure who knew how to feed myself three meals a day, balance a schedule of classes, not lock my keys inside the room (thankfully, and luckily, the residence hall staff would be able to lend me the spare key every so often to save myself each time I did), make friends, and take care of myself.

The first time I did laundry in the dorms, I put all of my dirty clothes in the dryer and wondered why they were still soapy—and warm. It took a few moments to realize the washer and dryer were not the same design as the ones at home, and I had mixed up the washer and the dryer. I felt like I had failed at being an independent adult, and that somehow my independent adult card would be revoked.

This feeling of independence being ripped away from young autistic people—especially those who spent their childhoods under the watchful eye of overprotective relatives or other trusted grown-ups—is not uncommon. An autistic friend of mine regularly stresses before his mother visits from out of town, ensuring his apartment is absolutely spotless so he does not feel overly criticized, and he fears a talking-to about his cleaning habits and priorities. He once told me he was afraid an inadequately clean and organized home would prompt an invitation demanding he move back home, in effect ripping him away from the life he spent his twenties working to build.

If I didn't feel independent at 18, even though I was living on my own and determined to find my future career and life path, when did that watershed moment come? Was it when I graduated, had my first job offer in hand, set up a retirement savings account, or began dating in earnest? Was it realizing, as the clichéd phrase goes, "I am a strong, independent woman who doesn't need a man?" I'm not really sure. Maybe there was no definite moment that screamed "independence" at me, but I did learn this: independence included thinking for myself, speaking on my own behalf (although sometimes with assistance from wonderful allies), and taking the initiative to do things or be able to ask for guidance.

DEFINING "INDEPENDENCE"

Since I can't pinpoint an exact moment when I felt independent, I thought I'd take a more literal approach to deciding what independence means for autistic people. To figure out what exactly *independence* means, I have explored all the tools at my disposal—the dictionary, my lived experience, my community. The dictionary says that being independent is not depending on another for livelihood or assistance. In the disability rights sphere, the Independent Living Movement is entirely rooted in concepts that autistic adults labor for each and every day. The independent living philosophy says we, as disabled people, are the experts on ourselves and should organize and advocate for ourselves individually and together, so we have better options and solutions for inclusion and full participation in society. Independence, then, is the freedom to ultimately make our own decisions.

Depending on who you ask, independence for people with disabilities ultimately boils down to having opportunities to make decisions that affect a person's life, the ability to pursue activities of a person's own choosing, with the only limitations being the same ones that nondisabled people face. We should be able to live where we want, with or without assistance, love who we want without penalty, apply for and hold jobs without fear of discrimination, and participate in our communities without barriers to access. Struggles towards independence for people with disabilities come in the form of barriers in everyday tasks and rites of passage in life, from transport issues, where we live and who we live with, employment, social activities and making friends, and our hobbies (REACH n.d.).

Think about what independence would mean to you. The following are some suggestions or ideas:

- Living on your own outside of your parents' house.

- Having a paying job or career you like.

- Managing your own money without assistance.

- Being able to make your own medical decisions.

- Not being under guardianship, thus being able to legally make your own decisions.

- Being in a romantic relationship with a partner of your choosing.

THE MYTH OF "DO IT ALL YOURSELF"

Feeling invincible is fairly common as a young autistic adult, especially when you have your first tastes of freedom or your self-advocacy is listened to and respected by virtue of the fact you are somehow an actual adult. And that fear of losing independence is also very real. For the longest time, I believed independence meant that you must do everything by yourself. The dictionary definitions of "independent" include being free from outside control or not depending on another person's authority, or not depending on another person for livelihood or assistance. With such literal interpretations and so much emphasis placed on independence as a goal for young autistic adults, the idea of requiring assistance in daily living or any sort of task creates this pressure that you have to be and do everything on your own.

Rather, for people with disabilities, "independence" as a strict dictionary definition of not needing others for assistance is a harmful assertion. Independence is a goal often celebrated by educators, parents, and disability support professionals alike, but what are we trying to be independent from? The way independence is phrased and talked about, you would think we were colonized people or nations seeking to break free from an oppressive regime. It leads to unrealistic expectations, so that when we do need help, we shy away from asking for it until we are so deeply entrenched in autistic burnout or having consistent meltdowns that we have no choice.

Doug Blecher, founder of Autism Personal Coach, provides coaching to autistic teens and adults. He has a different approach to the concept of independence. "Independent living is a fallacy, it doesn't exist," Blecher explains to me. "Every one of us needs help from others to navigate our daily lives. Living *interdependently* is the most likely way you will live your best autistic life."

Doug's words rang true for me and for others within the autistic and disability communities. Interdependence instead of independence seems a lot more realistic for all of us, regardless of neurology. As I have gotten older, I have learned more about how *interdependence* is a better goal for autistic and disabled adults. As disabled activists note, no one is truly independent in their lifetime—we all depend on someone or something for assistance, whether it is when we are newborn babies or if we become a famous movie star. Instead, interdependence recognizes that we, as people, are part of a community, and each of us is able to contribute to and receive assistance from the community. It acknowledges that there are things each of us, disabled, autistic, or nondisabled, are good at and not so good at. Interdependence allows us to lean on one another to give and receive the support we each need.

Mia Mingus, a disability justice activist, said in a talk in 2017 at the Paul K. Longmore Institute on Disability, that "interdependence moves us away from the myth of independence, and towards relationships where we are all valued and have things to offer. It moves us away from knowing disability only through 'dependence,' which paints disabled bodies as being a burden to others, at the mercy of able-bodied people's benevolence" (Mingus 2017). In other words, Mia is saying that disabled people are not just dependent people deserving of pity or a drain on society, but that they need to be supported and valued as individuals.

ASKING FOR HELP WHEN NEEDED

When talking about interdependence, Doug Blecher offered some extra advice:

> There isn't any one person who has all the answers, but asking people who may know the answers or have expertise in an area that you don't is an invaluable skill. When you can remind yourself that you don't have an answer to something and you can ask for help, it shows great strength.

True story: I hate asking for help. In school, it once took me until I failed a test to ask a teacher for help because I was afraid of how it would be perceived if I did not understand something (I later learned that asking for help in school was not a bad thing, that teachers and professors want their students to succeed, and that sometimes student failures meant there were miscommunications in teaching the material, so asking for help could also help educators improve too). I tend to avoid asking for assistance—even if I think I need it—unless something is either very wrong, I am very burned out, or I am feeling impossibly stuck. Like many, I am afraid of being seen as incompetent because there are such low expectations of autistic people in society, and I want to be seen as fully human, capable, and deserving of respect as humanly possible. It's taken me a long time—and it is ongoing—for me to recognize that asking for help is not a sign of weakness or something I'll be negatively judged for, but a sign of self-awareness and strength. Heck, sometimes in law practice, going at something without consulting with an expert or more senior lawyer can even be malpractice—asking for help is the smart thing to do.

There are certain things I do know I need to ask for help with no matter what. Unless you are a financial planner, a lawyer, a realtor, a landlord, a doctor, a mental health provider, and have all of the answers to each of your problems or to-do tasks in your brain, you probably also need help in at least one aspect of your life. That's okay! We all do!

Here's how I try to frame that "I need help" aspect. I am not an accountant, so I know chances are I will need to ask someone who knows more than I do about filing my taxes in compliance with what the Internal Revenue Service (IRS) (HM Revenue & Customs in the UK) requires, because I do not want to get into trouble or make a mistake. I am also not a realtor (estate agent), so I might not know where to go to find the perfect home if I were to move to a new area, or perhaps I don't know how to best negotiate for a lower monthly rent or begin the mortgaging process if I were to buy a house or an apartment. I also can't perform my annual physical or other medical exams on myself, so I need to make doctor's appointments; it also helps to have outsider perspectives on all aspects of my healthcare. An outsider might have unique solutions to any personal problems I may have. For all of these reasons, I know it is okay to have a village of people to help me be able to function and to run my life. The specialized groups of knowledge will be covered throughout the book, so you can find these key members of your personal village and succeed in communicating with them.

There are also interpersonal things autistic adults might need help with, too. Depending on your relationship with relatives and friends, you may confide in them with some of the daily challenges you face because you want to have the perspective of someone you trust, or you want a listening ear to help talk things through.

Even when this book was a mere idea, I knew I could not write it chock full of advice based solely on my own life experiences. To make this book the best it could be, I needed the help of other autistic adults who have done this "interdependent living" and "adulthood" thing, as well as other experts who work with autistic adults who have more insight and knowledge on more specific, nuanced topics than I do. Ultimately, having assistance allows us to have access to be our best selves and to do the best job we can at navigating the world.

AUTISTIC SELF-DISCOVERY

I was nine years old when I first found out I was autistic. At the time, I was obsessed with the Harry Potter books and movies—everything in my life revolved around the Wizarding World (my birthday party! Toys! I would be Hermione Granger for Halloween that year!) and character that also happened to share my July 31 birthday. That summer, my parents explained my autism diagnosis to me through Harry Potter—I was told I had magic in me, and, of course, being nine years old, I believed it. My mom explained to me, "Different is neither better nor worse. It's just different. And different could be extraordinary." Harry Potter was different than the folks he knew in the non-magical Muggle world because of his wizarding family, but he was also different from the other wizards because he was the famous boy who lived with that very apparent lightning bolt scar; I was different because I was able to see the world from a unique perspective, I was very creative and sensitive with a superior memory, and I didn't quite fit in with my peers.

My mom's words resonated with me for a long time. She was essentially preaching autistic acceptance and self-discovery early on. Following our discussion about Harry Potter, we talked about my strengths so I could become more confident in my autism diagnosis and begin building autistic identity. We talked about how I was sensitive, kind, creative, smart, and a good listener (I hope I am still all of these things). Then, we completed an autism workbook together that highlighted autistic traits. Discovering I was autistic did not solve the mystery for me of why I was "weird" or anything; as a kid, I always had high self-esteem. But to this day, autism helps explain why I am the way I am: certain personality traits, quirks, things I excel at and things I struggle with. Each day, I learn something new about how autism affects my life through shared autistic community and the piling challenges of getting older and growing as a person.

Not everyone has the privilege or access to a diagnosis in childhood, or family members who tell them about their autism at an early age in order to build autistic identity, confidence, and self-advocacy skills. Some autistic adults do not discover they are on the spectrum until their time as college students, or in their twenties, thirties, and beyond, through either diagnosis, research, or their children's diagnoses. Others find autistic community online and something clicks. Some autistic adults do not have access to a formal diagnosis because of where they live, the costs associated with an assessment, a lack of qualified clinicians, or personal choices not to seek out a professional assessment for autism. Regardless of whether someone is formally diagnosed with autism, self-discovery and autistic identity building are part of the autistic experience.

Find autistic community

For young autistic people, feeling isolated or alone is not an abnormal sensation. On average, one in three young people on the autism spectrum experience social isolation (Orsmond *et al.* 2013). Social isolation can mean a lot of things—not having anyone to hang out with (or choosing to be completely alone), not receiving messages from others either by phone or online, only receiving digital communication and having a lack of face-to-face interaction, or wanting to be part of something but being excluded. Perhaps you felt alone growing up or during your early school years, or all of your friends were neurotypical, so you felt somewhat like an outsider, having to mask and suppress autistic traits.

My first introduction to autistic community was when I was

13 years old and was invited to speak on a panel at the Autism Society of America annual conference back in 2008. While the panel was a life-changing experience that taught me how much I enjoyed autistic advocacy and giving back, the real gem of the conference for me was meeting other, older autistic adults. The first autistic young adult friend I made was Brigid Rankowski, an autistic advocate who, at the time, was a college student. I immediately felt a sense of kinship and hope—Brigid was the first autistic college student I had ever known, and it was the moment I felt like I was not alone and could do things like go to college away from home when I was older. After scheduled conference events, Brigid and other autistics would gather, and I was part of the group that hung out with them socially at the pool or around the hotel. It was the first autistic kinship I experienced, and certainly not the last time I felt a semblance of autistic community.

Local community support groups

After the Autism Society conference in 2008, I did not know anyone who was openly autistic in my high school, and nor was I part of a local support group. I came out and shared I was autistic to my neurotypical peers during my freshman year of high school (Year 10 in the UK); they seemed receptive and would later go on to applaud my bravery, but the act itself did not change my social life whatsoever or connect me with other autistic students.

The only time I went to a support group was through my university's on-campus disability center several years later, and I walked away feeling out of place and uncomfortable. The group was led by a neurotypical staff member and focused on a very specific topic for the week; it escapes my mind if it was on socializing or academic stressors, but the interactions between all of us autistic folks felt very awkward and forced because of this guidance and leadership from the neurotypical group leader. I wanted nothing more than to talk to a senior architecture major in the group because she was in a sorority,[1] and I wanted to ask more about how accepting the house was and how she was navigating the social minefield of the recruitment process because it was something I had decided against, thinking it would be too overwhelming, though I desperately wanted to have a group of friends. The support group somehow did not allow for those connections to naturally unfold. However, autism research at universities and inclusion for autistic students have evolved since I was an undergraduate. Some local or college groups may be autistic-led or based in a neurodiversity or disability center. Those groups with neurodivergent facilitators or a positive setting may provide more peer support or a feeling of community.

Check within a campus, meetup sites, or social media for something more informal, or local autistic advocacy groups or autism nonprofits to see what adult groups may be available in case having an in-person or regional group of autistic peers is helpful in giving you a sense of shared identity and community. My local autism organizations and others around the country host support groups and a community space for autistic adults, with some particularly focusing on women, LGBTQ+ autistics, job seekers, or young adults. See what best suits your needs— and if you're feeling brave, you might choose to start your own group, too.

It's a small neurodiverse world after all: finding online support

We are not controlled by where we live. If you live in a small town or do not live near a major university, or do not feel

---

1   For more information on sororities (and fraternities), see https://en.wikipedia.org/wiki/Fraternities_and_sororities

comfortable connecting locally or in person, the internet is teeming with support options (I have included a list of online resources at the end of the book). I did not know while growing up or even until later on about the robustness of the online autistic community.

The history of the conventional autistic and neurodiversity movement points to autistic organizing and community occurring online beginning in the late 1990s. At some point in my teen years, I regularly read threads on Wrong Planet, a blog and web-based forum where autistics, parents, and professionals would post about different aspects in their lives, from making friends, love and dating, work, school, or their special interests, to meeting new people with similar experiences. While I never signed up for Wrong Planet, I felt comforted reading the anecdotes of other autistic people, and reassured that there was indeed a whole bunch of people out there who were the same version of different that I was.

Places like Wrong Planet are more common now than ever. Autistic community online—locally, nationally, or internationally—is far wider reaching, nuanced, and more accessible than in the days of the early internet or more specialized websites like Wrong Planet. There are no shortages of Facebook groups for autistic people, Tumblr posts and blogs about autism, Discord servers dedicated to neurodiversity and autistic gamers, and, of course, the vastness of autistic Twitter.

Finding community is associated with a stronger sense of identity, support, and belonging. Online community is a powerful tool for friendships, support, and coalition building—if you use it wisely and safely.

Hashtag autism: finding your people

Autistic Twitter in particular is a valuable resource and community pillar for both autistic and neurotypical folks alike.

A search of #AskingAutistics nets questions from parents and professionals trying to learn more about the issues that autistic adults face as well as their experiences alongside peer support in the vein of "Is this a me thing or is this an everyone on the spectrum thing?" Meanwhile, hashtags like #ActuallyAutistic and #AllAutistics are used to signal that the speaker or writer is also on the autism spectrum and to find others to relate and share with. Autistic Twitter is also more intersectional, with specific hashtags and subcommunities to cater towards multiply marginalized folks, including autistics of color, LGBTQ+ autistics, and women and nonbinary people. I have made several autistic friends through the Twitterverse, bonding over shared life experiences, adapting to the world around us, and facing the same challenges day in, day out.

However, if you're looking for community online, be sure to *practice internet safety to protect your personal information and privacy.* Think about whether or not your social media profiles are public and if the support groups you join are public too. If you aren't comfortable or do not want to publicly disclose you're autistic (because a future employer might see it, for instance), sign up for autism-related social media under a pseudonym or screen name to protect your identity. Do not reveal too much personal and identifying information about where you live and go to school or work, and do not meet anyone offline unless others are aware of when and where you are going and who you will be with, that it is in a public place in case something happens, and others are able to observe, and you feel safe and comfortable. More about online safety will be covered in the dating section of this book (under "Socializing"), given the popularity of meeting romantic and sexual partners through the internet.

Recognize autistic and disability identity are individual journeys

Often, after I talk about my own story, listeners are quick to point out that I seem so confident in being autistic, and either a parent or a young autistic person will ask me how I feel so much pride in who I am since they have either been teased, bullied, or otherwise rejected or feel ashamed of their autism. I think I am lucky that I have generally always been very confident because I have very positive parents and role models in my life and always felt affirmed in my identity, but identity is not a perfect, smooth road for everyone.

Truth is, autistic and disability identity is a messy, complicated thing, often due to the messaging surrounding autism as well as ableism and internalized ableism. *Ableism* is a prejudice against people with disabilities that can look like discrimination or being treated negatively because of disability. It can be overt, such as denying access to an event or an accommodation, thus excluding you on the basis of autism. Or it can be subtle, unexplained bias that you experience.

Ableism can also be veiled with good intentions. Some of my earliest experiences involve what I call *benevolent ableism*, where people are well intentioned and want to be inclusive but miss the mark entirely by denying me the ability to make my own decisions. Given this book is about independence, self-determination, and self-advocacy, it feels shameful to admit that oftentimes our allies can be the ones who deny us agency and the ability to self-advocate. With benevolent ableism, exclusion happens at the hands of the people who regularly assure me that they love and care about me (Moss 2019). Friends might choose not to invite me to group outings because they think I might have a sensory overload, rather than let me make the decision myself. It makes me feel worse because they have my best interests at heart but they are robbing me of autonomy or thinking they know my autism better than they do—or worse, making me think deep down that they didn't invite me because they don't want to deal with something like a sensory processing difference.

Internalized ableism is subtler and can particularly impact a person's self-esteem. It's when people with disabilities believe the negative messaging surrounding their disability, see themselves as less worthy, and act accordingly. Some thoughts we might have relating to internalized ableism are thinking things like "I'm not good enough," "I will never get a job," "I am broken and need to be fixed," or "I am asking for too much" because of autism. Ableism and internalized ableism can impact our self-esteem in not very pleasant ways.

For me, internalized ableism looks like believing I might be burdening others if I ask for accommodations or if we go to a different restaurant for dinner because of my autism-related food aversions or the potential for a sensory overload. Sometimes it is believing I am lazy when I struggle with executive functioning tasks. For others, internalized ableism might be adapting coping strategies like increased masking and camouflaging to attempt to appear more neurotypical, in order to feel or appear less autistic to gain acceptance and validation from others and from within. Either way, these types of behaviors and beliefs about autistic people and how we feel about ourselves can lead to all sorts of hard feelings in young adulthood and throughout our lives, and it takes active work to unlearn the stigmatizing things we are taught by others and our society.

This is where the concept of *neurodiversity* comes into play. The term "neurodiversity" was coined in 1998 by Judy Singer, an Australian sociologist who is on the autism spectrum, who believes that a diversity of neurological wiring and brain function is a naturally occurring variation. Neurodiversity is a concept where neurological differences are to be recognized and respected as any other human variation. Autistic people are not the only ones who need neurodiversity; neurodivergence also includes our friends with attention-deficit hyperactivity disorder (ADHD), learning disabilities, mental health disabilities, and neurological disabilities.

While I am proud to be autistic and talk about it along with neurodiversity fairly often, I am actively working to remind myself I am not burdening others or am less competent when I honor my disability-related access needs. Why wouldn't I want to put in the work towards equity and genuine inclusion to be accepted, loved, and appreciated as my full self?

"You get proud by practicing"

I find comfort in the wisdom of autistic and disabled elders, or people who have similar disabilities who are older than me or who were our ancestors and who are no longer alive but left behind knowledge, writing, words, or had another profound impact. One of those pieces of wisdom from an ancestor sums up disability and autistic identity for me. It's a poem by disability rights activist Laura Hershey (1962–2010), aptly titled "You get proud by practicing." Laura taught me that pride is something you have to learn and practice feeling. The final stanza of her poem refers to the idea of others making you feel ashamed, and that it's up to you to feel pride in yourself. Other people and society will send messages that might make you second-guess or feel ashamed or insecure about being autistic and disabled because they see these identities as confusing, or weak, or misunderstand them. This includes ableism and internalized ableism. Ultimately, self-esteem and confidence come from within, and that also includes owning all the parts of who you are, including autism and its status as both difference and disability.

The evolution of language and self

It is very difficult to spend time in any autism- or disability-related space without having a debate over language and how to describe autism. Are we autistic or do we have autism? Are we high functioning or severely autistic? What about Asperger's? And what about broader disability-related language like "disabled" or "special needs"?

Throughout this book, I mostly use identity-first language, referring to us as "autistic" or "neurodivergent." Language relating to autism primarily falls into two camps: person-first and identity-first. Educators and professionals are taught to use person-first language like "people with autism" to show respect and to emphasize an individual's humanity. Identity-first language uses the disability as a defining characteristic, and this is what happens when we call ourselves "autistic" or "disabled." Not everyone uses identity-first language because they see words like "disabled" or "autistic" as bad or offensive. Somewhere in the middle, perhaps unique to autism, is "on the autism spectrum." As another autistic person described to me, "'on the autism spectrum' is the Switzerland of language"—citing its inoffensive nature and that not many people outright prefer the term. Euphemisms for disability or autism are unhelpful for describing ourselves and do not typically begin within our community, but with well-meaning allies who are uncomfortable saying "disability"—hence we get terms like "special needs," "special abilities," "diffability," and "differently-abled."

Claire Barnett, an autistic self-advocate who works at Vanderbilt University's Frist Center for Autism and Innovation, sparked a social media campaign about how "disabled" is not a bad word. To contribute to that conversation, self-advocates embraced their disabled identity in posts with graphics Barnett provided to share. I explained in my post that "disabled" is a sense of pride, culture, and identity for me.

While language continually evolves, so does how we describe

ourselves individually. I did not always identify as disabled, or even autistic—I used to use different language because of what I thought was correct at the time. In my teenage years, I identified as having high-functioning autism because that was my diagnosis, and I wanted to separate myself from an Asperger syndrome label since I had not been diagnosed with Asperger's. I later learned about how high functioning and low functioning separated our community and identities—people would write off my challenges since I did not "look autistic," while folks who were seen as low functioning would have their abilities and strengths written off or called into question. Instead, I have begun using "support needs" and describing what help and support people with more significant disabilities may need so I do not discount what my fellow autistic and disabled siblings are capable of—or dismiss the challenges others face.

So, as I got older, I began to see my wonderful, complicated full autistic identity, and how that also fitted into the greater disability community. It turned out I wasn't largely disabled by autism, but I was disabled by society's attitudes, the ableist systems of oppression society upholds, and a lack of inclusion and accessibility.

How we talk about ourselves matters. Some people prefer to refer to themselves as autistic, people with autism, on the spectrum, or as having Asperger's. How someone identifies is entirely up to them, and we should be respectful of their preferences. As autistic folks, we have the right to decide how we talk about ourselves—and for others to respect those choices, whether or not they fully agree with them.

"Perfect in an imperfect world": evaluating strengths and weaknesses

When I was first told about my autism, the focus was almost solely on my strengths—that was, nine-year-old me would not feel insecure about being autistic and different from her peers. Unlike a lot of young autistic people, I did not think I was weird or awkward compared with neurotypical kids. I knew I would be the only one in class who was not invited to birthday parties or that I struggled befriending other girls my age, but I grew up believing I was the cool one, and they were weird for not inviting me or realizing how great a friend I could be. As a family friend explained to me when I was in my pre-teen years, I was "perfect in an imperfect world." In essence, I was exactly who I was meant to be, and there was nothing wrong with that, though the world is not exactly where it should be in terms of acceptance, inclusion, and making space for people who are different. But it isn't always my job to make the world perfect, or to make other people perfect in this imperfect world one at a time. Sometimes, in order to adapt, we have to take a good, hard look at ourselves—and the very things that make us who we are.

Here's the thing: you are perfect the way you are. Sure, we all have room for improvement, but you are not trying to become a neurotypical adult. We are always growing and trying to be the absolute best we can be for ourselves and for those around us. One of the ways we acknowledge who we are is to take stock of our strengths and weaknesses. Doing this is an exercise in humility and self-awareness that allows us to evaluate what we enjoy and what we dislike as well as who we are as individuals.

Sometimes our strengths are skills and talents and qualities we have that other people admire. For instance, whenever I am asked about my strengths, I think about my personal and professional life. I consider my hobbies, interests, and who I am as a person, and reflect back on the aspects of myself that my parents highlighted when they first told me I was autistic. I think I am a good listener; I am also resilient, creative, empathetic, and curious. At work, I can thoroughly analyse issues and connect with others in a way that they feel I am trustworthy. As far as weaknesses, I think about how I wish sometimes I had more patience and was more organized, I am not as technologically savvy as some of the autism stereotypes suggest, I am not super-athletic, and sometimes I am honest to a fault. These things create a map for me of things I would be good at and also how to be a better friend and person—it tells me I do not belong in data-driven jobs, I need to be challenged, I have some struggles with executive functioning, and I can also benefit from slowing down to consider how other people feel if I say something too unfiltered or my lack of patience shines through in a way that may hurt someone else's feelings.

To start this process, it can help to write out a list of things you like about yourself or you are good at. You can also ask friends and family for qualities they admire about you (but also be prepared to give them a compliment and tell them what you admire about them!). And then, face the honesty of things you could improve on or wish you were better at. This is also a wonderful segue into caring for your mental health and self-discovery as well.

Self-Care: Not Just Bubble Baths and Special Interests

True story: I spend too much time scrolling through Instagram, and because I work in the disability space and have an undergraduate degree in psychology, I get inundated with mental health and overall wellness content, often with calming words and messaging about "self-care." It can be irritating since I'll be expecting to check out what my friends are up to, and instead I'll be reading about how we can honor our boundaries or see some very fit person relaxing on a beach or doing yoga.

It wasn't until fairly recently I had even heard of "self-care," and when I had, I first thought it related to grooming and hygiene. Of course I can take care of myself: I can shower, brush my teeth, blow dry my hair, maybe get a manicure and a pedicure, and put on clothes I find comfortable and cute. Not a problem, except that this isn't actually what self-care means.

Eventually, my understanding evolved into a *Parks and Recreation*-style "treat yo self" (in the show, two of the characters have a day each year to relax where they treat themselves to anything they want—mostly expensive purchases and pampering themselves at the spa—and one of their colleagues joins in and only wants to buy and wear a Batman costume because it makes him happy).

Self-care looks different for us autistic people. It isn't treating ourselves by spending lots of money on things that bring us joy or spending a day at a luxurious spa. Self-care can include preventative actions that will help us avoid meltdowns and autistic burnout, like giving ourselves time to stim or creating and following a routine. Setting personal boundaries in social and professional situations can help us feel affirmed and respected as our autistic selves and prevent burnout or too much pressure to mask that would otherwise exhaust us.

Self-care needs and desires change for me each and every day. I try to find an hour a day to dedicate solely to myself in order to stay grounded and happy. For me, that can look like getting some exercise, playing a video game, talking to a friend, taking a bath, reading a book, going for a swim, or falling asleep an hour early or sleeping in. I do my best to listen to what my mind and body need each day in order to unwind and relax. This hour a day (and sometimes more on weekends or if I need it) helps keep me grounded and mentally healthy and energized to face whatever is ahead of me!

MONITORING YOUR MENTAL HEALTH

Reality check: autistic people have high rates of co-occurring mental health conditions and other neurodivergences like ADHD, depression, and anxiety. According to a recent study, 20.1 percent of autistic adults have a diagnosable anxiety disorder (Nimmo-Smith *et al.* 2020), and studies repeatedly show that depression diagnoses are also not uncommon for people on the autism spectrum (Hudson, Hall, and Harkness 2019). This means being honest and checking in with yourself, and taking care of your mental health should be a top priority.

We all experience crises, stressful events, and ups and downs with our feelings and states of mind. We are not completely numb, and nor are we permanently happy all of the time. We are not robots. We may also have a lot of feelings because contrary to popular belief, autistic people are incredibly empathetic, often taking on others' emotions and experiencing them first-hand as well.

You would not neglect your physical health or hesitate to rest or go to a doctor if you were physically not feeling well. You should give your brain the same level of attention, alertness, and care that you give your body.

Managing stress and anxiety

Life is stressful. We have a lot of responsibilities as adults, additional burdens to bear as autistic people, and juggle roles that we have at home, school, and/or work. Too much stress can cause anxiety, meltdowns, or autistic burnout. We may also become stressed not due to events in our lives, but due to the world we live in. Sensory overloads are stressful. Meltdowns are stressful. Not fully understanding neurotypical communication is stressful. Being a target of bullying and intolerance is stressful. It is no wonder anxiety and stress are common for us autistic folks, but we can manage them with some activities and ways to check in with ourselves.

I am regularly stressed because I have a lot of responsibilities and obligations in my personal and professional life. If I get too stressed, I become irritable with those I care about and inadvertently upset them.

- *Deal with the stressful thing head on.* If one particular situation or responsibility is stressing you out and it is within your control, tackling the problem head on can ease stress because you won't spend extra time just thinking about it. Sometimes thinking is worse than doing. You've got this!

- *Recognize you need time for yourself.* Being "on" all the time can be exhausting. Social interactions—especially with neurotypical people—can lead to increased masking and camouflaging, both of which take their mental toll on autistic people attempting to find acceptance and to assimilate in order to avoid bullying, exclusion, or other external consequences in an unaccepting society (Hull *et al.* 2017). According to researchers, masking is taking on a persona that is felt to be more neurotypical, while camouflaging is hiding behavior that might be viewed as socially unacceptable, or "performing" social behavior that is felt to be more neurotypical (Attwood 2007; Lai *et al.* 2017).

- *Know it is okay to say "no."* Dr Lori Butts, my co-host on the *Spectrumly Speaking* podcast, spoke with me about stress management on the show in August 2019. During our conversation, she brought up a point that young people in particular are afraid to say "no" because they want to be seen as ambitious, reliable, and dependable, especially in workplace settings. There is also a fear that saying "no" socially means you'll be excluded in the future or seen as an unreliable friend. Setting this boundary as a way to calm down is crucial. Sometimes, friends might want to unload their personal problems and drama onto me because I am a good listener, and if it stresses me out, I try to say something like, "Hey, as much as I want to be here for you right now and help you, can I call you later? I'm also a little overwhelmed," and usually they understand that sometimes I have to put my own needs first. Sometimes, the things we say "yes" to without thinking are the things that put pressure on us or unnecessarily add to our stress loads. You are not unreliable or unworthy for choosing to prioritize your own mental health and wellbeing.

- *Spend an hour each day doing something you want to do to unwind.* This strategy in particular is a multipurpose one: (1) you might get to enjoy a special interest or hobby; (2) it might help you chill and relax; and (3) if you do this thing before bed, you might get some really good sleep that night.

What makes your mind completely dissociate from responsibilities so that you forget there is an outside world for a little while? For me, it can depend on the day. I completely forget about all my responsibilities when I watch new episodes of reality TV—it isn't too intense, it's lighthearted, and so detached from my experiences with producer-manufactured drama that I am able to feel the tenseness leave my body and to laugh a little bit. Some days, a nice bubble bath with some pleasing smells or a bath bomb before bedtime can put my body and mind at ease. Or I'll spend time with something I truly love, like dancing in my bedroom to Taylor Swift, playing a video game, or curling up to read a good novel.

Autistic burnout

Ever experience exhaustion so big that all of a sudden you might melt down, lose skills, and feel emotionally, mentally, or physically drained for days or weeks at a time? This is what researchers and autistic adults identify as *autistic burnout*, a term used to describe "a state of incapacitation, exhaustion, and distress in every area of life" (Raymaker *et al.* 2020). Adults who experience autistic burnout may experience a regression in skills or might appear more autistic to an unsuspecting neurotypical due to an inability to mask or communicate in line with society's largely neurotypical standards.

Dora Raymaker, an autistic researcher, along with her team, pioneered new research defining autistic burnout along with solutions to survive this intense sensation that is part of the autistic experience. In their study, they gave six domains for potential solutions and support related to burnout: "(1) acceptance and social support; (2) being autistic; (3) formal support; (4) reduced load; (5) self-knowledge; and (6) self-advocacy" (Raymaker *et al.* 2020, Table 3). Community support strategies include receiving care from loved ones, from others within the autistic community, or from professionals. Other strategies include listening to our own bodies and minds by communicating, setting, and honoring boundaries, pulling back socially, spending time with our hobbies and interests, or doing anything that makes us feel better about who we are or so we are able to recharge our mental and physical batteries.

I realize my biggest triggers for autistic burnout are too much stress and pressure I put on myself, so in order for me to avoid feeling so overwhelmed that I can't function, it is crucial that I set boundaries. Autistic burnout for me can be all-consuming exhaustion, and finding ways to prevent it by figuring out the triggers has helped me greatly.

I am someone who likes to do everything and does not want to disappoint anyone by declining to volunteer or help on projects when possible. Learning to say "no" when I have a lot of other competing commitments has been a lifesaver and a great way to care for myself, especially once I realized that the majority of people are fairly understanding and do not expect me to be superwoman (although sometimes they think I am anyway). I also figured out it is important for me to set aside alone time to spend with my special interests or do something I find relaxing at least once a day in order to feel calm and avoid that point of stress. I also try to take stock of tasks and commitments to see what is most pressing, so I can prioritize whenever possible.

Autistic burnout is a very real phenomenon that can leave us feeling depleted and frustrated, but proper support that helps you as well as recognizing its triggers can help avoid future burnouts.

Normalizing therapy

After being a psychology major, one of the most surprising things people hear me say is that I genuinely believe everyone—yes, everyone—can benefit from receiving counseling or some form of psychotherapy. Each of us could use an objective, nonjudgmental person in our lives who is able to help us sort through life's most difficult moments, conflicts, relationships, or different aspects of our past so they don't affect our future. It is not a bad thing to need support or to have a nonjudgmental sounding board.

So many folks I knew were afraid of going to receive counseling services, especially when I was in law school, because of the stigma of possibly being labeled with a mental health condition or having to report it to a state bar association as part of a "fit to practice" law screening. However, since I was at law school, the state bar associations now encourage counseling for stress and anxiety, and view therapy as management and treatment for more limiting and profound mental health disabilities.

For the rest of us, therapy or mental health counseling might be an option to help maintain our emotional wellbeing, work through problems, gain and use new problem-solving strategies, grow as people, or just have a professional person to rant or "infodump" to about the stresses or roadblocks we face in our daily lives.

Why might you want to go to therapy?

- You might want to talk out or solve a problem.

- You might be dealing with a lot of stress, anxiety, and/or depression.

- You might have lost a loved one (grief counseling).

- You are fighting with your romantic partner (couple's counseling).

- You are newly diagnosed as autistic, are self-diagnosed, or questioning if you are autistic or neurodivergent.

- You would like support and some strategies for autistic traits or challenges you face.

These are just a few suggestions or reasons why you might decide mental health counseling can be particularly helpful. There might be a reason not listed here that resonates with you as to why you should seek help or continue to seek help on a regular basis.

Finding a neurodiversity-affirming therapist

Finding a therapist or psychological services provider might be more of a journey for you because of your autism. Not all clinicians are well versed in disability. You might want someone who has particular experience with autistic clients because they understand your unique experiences and support needs, and are less likely to push neurotypical standards on you or require you to engage in the labor of educating them about autism and each nuance of your perspective from the ground up. It is valid to believe that you should not be shouldering the emotional burden of doing a full ableism, accessibility, and autism primer in the first few appointments or on a continuing basis.

It is okay if the first psychologist or therapist you meet with is not a good fit. Finding the right mental health provider is a journey and requires effort, but the right person will make you feel affirmed, heard, and seen. To help find a good fit, you should *research* therapists, *interview* them on their background, fees and costs, treatment philosophies, knowledge and expertise, and look to see if you have a good *rapport* since you might open up about things that may otherwise make you feel uncomfortable (Emamzadeh 2020). On the website of Dr Finn Gratton, an autistic and nonbinary psychotherapist, he elaborates on the importance of the interview phase for autistic people and those who support them: "questions about training and style are especially important in areas, such as transgender issues, eating disorders, and neurodiversity, which require more ongoing training and collaboration with other health and social service professionals" (Gratton n.d.). Basically, neurodiversity and autism are likely a part of your identity as a person and should be taken into account in your overall care.

Depending on what you're looking for, and as part of your research and interviewing, you might also want someone who is not only affirming of neurodiversity, but of your other identities as well. Perhaps in addition to being autistic, you also are a member of the LGBTQ+ community, a trauma survivor, or a person of color—or you exist at the intersection of many forms of marginalization. In that case, you may want a therapist who specializes in working with queer folks or trauma survivors, or it may be that you feel more comfortable seeking a therapist of color. Finding someone who is nonjudgmental, understanding, and professional means that you might be researching and interviewing for longer, but it also might be that the person who is the best fit also shares one or more of your identities—that way, they might have that innate understanding of what it is like to exist and navigate this world in a certain way.

When I spoke to Dr Gratton for an interview on the *Spectrumly Speaking* podcast, I was able to imagine just how profound their understanding of the neurodivergent experience must be for clients, especially those who are neurodivergent, traumatized, and transgender or nonbinary as well. Speaking to autistic professionals across all fields is a validating feeling.

Visiting a therapist's office may also be scary due to the sensory nature or a pressure to mask in an unfamiliar environment. Some psychological service providers offer telehealth or virtual appointments, and platforms like BetterHelp and Talkspace allow users to be connected with licensed counselors, psychologists, and social workers in their state (or county) online for video sessions and text messaging support.

What about cost?

Counseling and mental healthcare options may also be available for you at a low cost due to your health insurance plan, an Employee Assistance Plan (EAP), or university setting (often free for students), or you might be able to come to an arrangement with a provider in order to lower the cost of mental health services. Online-only providers like BetterHelp and Talkspace may be cheaper but might not be reimbursable through your health insurance. Make sure to research costs and fees, and also to ask therapists up front when you first consult with them.

Medication

A therapist might refer you to a psychiatrist, a medical doctor who can prescribe medication to help manage neurodivergent traits or mental health issues. This might include antidepressants, anti-anxiety medication, or other antipsychotic or mood-altering medication. Be sure to communicate with your healthcare providers about dosage, side effects, or complications, and see how the medication impacts your mood, functioning, or other areas of your wellbeing. There is nothing to be ashamed of in needing medicine to manage your mental health.

If you are in danger

If you are in the middle of a mental health crisis and are struggling with thoughts of hurting yourself or others, those in the US should reach out immediately to the National Suicide Prevention Lifeline at any time for free and confidential support on 1-800-273-8255. In the UK, the Shout Crisis Text Line will connect you via text 24/7 when you text "SHOUT" to 85258; if you'd rather call a hotline, you can call the Samaritans at any time on 116 123. For those of you in different countries, look up similar crisis hotlines and support organizations.

KEY TAKEAWAYS

- It's okay if you need support and help, whether it is from loved ones, community members, mental health professionals, or a crisis care hotline.

- Realizing what causes stress and anxiety can help prevent autistic burnout or a major mental health event.

- Take care of yourself! This looks different for each autistic person. Figure out what relaxes you and brings joy into your life.

HEALTHCARE AND DOCTORS

Mental health is only the beginning or an added bonus in the web of taking care of yourself—then there's getting care for your physical health.

I dread going to the doctors for a variety of different reasons—I don't always know what they are going to do, or switching doctors for any reason can also be scary (throughout my life I had to switch physicians because I aged out of my pediatrician, graduated from a university, or moved away from home so I wanted care closer to where I lived). I also wrestle with how to talk about autism with a new physician—disclosing can allow for negative treatment and stereotyping, build trust, or allow an autistic patient to receive reasonable accommodations to make the appointment less overwhelming. One of the first times I went to a healthcare provider alone, I disclosed my autism and watched the physician's assistant note in my chart that autism "was something I had in childhood," and realized advocating for my healthcare needs had become even more of an uphill battle than if I hadn't disclosed or had a support person with me. Others thanked me for letting them know and asked me to let them know what I may need to make the appointment run as smoothly as possible.

Silvia Gil, who heads up adult service programs at the University of Miami-Nova Southeastern University Center for Autism & Related Disabilities, is part of the team that provides "autism-friendly" designations to businesses, organizations, and healthcare providers in the South Florida area. For them, it is all about training and making it so providers are aware of autism, recognizing what autism looks like in adults and children, and how to best accommodate and communicate with us.

Regardless of training, there are certain things providers can do to make healthcare more accessible to autistic adult patients:

- *Treat autistic adults like adults.* This should go without saying, but it is extremely frustrating when an autism diagnosis is mentioned in a medical appointment and the provider immediately treats me—or any autistic adult—like a child. We may communicate differently with assisted communication or use more body language or have varied processing speeds, but that does not mean we are unable to understand what a provider is talking about. It is okay to ask if something makes sense or if there is a better way to explain something, or to use lay terms for complicated medical jargon.

For autistic patients, sometimes you might have to give either a gentle or stern reminder that you are an adult who is able to manage your own care. It is one of the many ways we can self-advocate and ensure we are treated with respect.

- *Be considerate of access needs. Access needs* refer to what a person needs to communicate, learn, and take part in an activity (Pacific Alliance on Disability Self-Advocacy 2016). Everyone has access needs—practitioners included—in order to make an environment and appointment manageable and accessible.

  Physicians have a professional responsibility to treat patients of all abilities with respect. They should not make fun of autistic patients or deny them accommodations that might make the appointment doable for them, including, but not limited to, telehealth options, bringing a support person, having sensory aids, or requesting clear communication.

  My access needs include having everything explained to me to avoid anxiety, even if that procedure or thing being explained might seem like common sense or not worth explaining. No matter how trite a person's needs may seem, they are to be accepted and reasonably accommodated.

- *Communicate clearly and thoroughly.* I always ask doctors to share what they are going to be doing before they do it. It helps me to relax and anticipate what will happen next. Sometimes this can be as simple as being told I will be receiving a necessary vaccine on the count of three, or showing me a specific tool that will be used to measure a bodily function. With clear communication,

I know exactly what I am consenting to and they are not minimizing a major procedure or blowing a routine exam out of proportion, and if something makes me feel uncomfortable, I can properly advocate for myself beforehand or in the moment.

To make sure autistic adults understand what is happening, *plain language* is a great place to start with communicating, especially for autistics who have more significant support needs or may also have a co-occurring intellectual disability. Plain language is a tool that puts complex concepts into easy-to-understand wording. It is not the same as explaining to a child, but instead, losing the medical jargon and putting what is happening into ordinary terms so anybody could understand what is happening. Plain language can be a helpful tool in communicating with autistics not just in the medical field, but more broadly.

The maintenance cheat sheet of doctors you should see

If you absolutely dread going to doctors, here are appointments you should probably make part of your annual routine, just to make sure everything is working properly—appointments with a family physician, a gynecologist, and a dentist. Depending on your health insurance, some of these visits can be completely covered at no extra cost. If you have any other mental or physical health conditions, you may need to visit specialists—be sure to check out the "Monitoring Your Mental Health" section of this chapter for tips about finding neurodiversity-affirming providers for counseling and psychiatric services (see "Self-Care").

- *A family physician/general practitioner.* Everyone should have one main doctor they trust, typically a general practitioner or family doctor. This is the person you go to for a routine physical health check, who can order and run bloodwork, and, depending on the demands of your health insurance or other doctors, may be the one who refers you to more specialized doctors for various ailments and procedures beyond what happens from routine screenings, bloodwork, or an annual physical.

To find a family doctor you trust, if you are newly 18, you might start by asking your pediatrician for a referral. College students may continue seeing their pediatrician depending on the practice, or may elect to use their college or university's student health options. You might ask friends about their experiences, search the internet, or see if any of your local autism organizations have a network for referrals and suggestions for providers who have experience with autistic adults.

- *A gynecologist (if you have a uterus).* If you were born female and have a uterus and are in your twenties or thirties, seeing a gynecologist annually (sometimes more often or less, depending on your unique health profile) is important because that way, you can be screened for cervical cancer, have a pap smear, receive testing for sexually transmitted diseases, and also discuss options in your sexual and reproductive health such as contraception, if you are planning on becoming pregnant or having children, are currently pregnant, or if you have additional concerns. You may need to see a gynecologist more often if you have additional complications or have side effects as a result of prescribed contraceptive solutions, or need a refill on a prescription.

  To find a safe, inclusive gynecologist or intimate care provider, the Autistic Women & Nonbinary Network (AWN) hosts a database and survey that autistic people complete to share who in their state or area has had positive experiences with sensory-friendly providers.

- *A dentist.* Going to the dentist is a sensory onslaught for autistic people, from the office and tools to the uncomfortable positions your mouth is open in. You may have past trauma from dental visits in childhood that makes you want to avoid going as an adult. As a rule of thumb, dentists recommend having a clean and checkup every six months, although some people may need to go more often or less, based on how healthy their teeth and mouth are, or if they have other underlying conditions.

  To make going to a dentist easier, try to find ways to distract yourself from what is happening. A good dentist will explain what they are doing as thoroughly as possible if you want them to, in order to reduce anxiety. To minimize sensory input, wear headphones, watch videos, play games, or have a conversation going (as best you can, and if you want), to avoid focusing on the procedure or mouth exam at hand.

  Of course, to avoid having to go to the dentist more than necessary, it is important to practice good hygiene by brushing your teeth twice a day and flossing—although you should make an appointment if you are in pain or have any other issues.

- *A psychiatrist.* If you are receiving medication for mental health symptoms, a psychiatrist is the doctor who will write you a prescription for treatment of mental health disabilities and symptoms. At first, you might see them frequently to see how a new medication is working, but after that, you might check in with them annually, or if you need different medicines to manage your mental health.

The self-advocacy perspective

To make doctors' appointments easier, Chloe Rothschild, an autistic self-advocate from Ohio, has a few tips and recommendations for autistic patients (2020):

- *Take a trusted caretaker or friend with you to the appointment to help you advocate.* Chloe recommends taking someone with you to help with self-advocacy, if you feel comfortable sharing medical information with this person, whether they are a caregiver, relative, or friend. Unfortunately, not all doctors take people with disabilities seriously—this can also be further impacted by other forms of marginalization—and sometimes, having an ally in the room can ensure your needs are met. Chloe also says that this person can help you understand and remember what the doctor said after the appointment, which can be particularly helpful if you receive a lot of information at once, feel overwhelmed, or have a meltdown.

- *Bring sensory tools and/or items to keep you calm while waiting for your appointment or to bring into the appointment.* If you have a favorite compact stim toy or fidget, take it with you if it will help you feel less nervous.

- *Write out a list of questions or concerns or program them onto a communication device ahead of time.* My mom always used to recommend this to me as well, because I would get nervous or blank out when the doctor started talking, and would often go to an appointment for a very specific reason or a litany of little things which I wasn't sure how concerned to be about. Writing down questions might help folks feel less nervous or also ensure their communication preferences are taken seriously. Chloe also recommends writing out a list of medications and symptoms to bring along with the questions and concerns so you know what to cover or talk about when the doctor is in the room with you.

Miscellaneous must-haves

I recommend having an "emergency plan" or document written out somewhere with all of the important information you might need in order to reduce cognitive load and keep all of your healthcare information straight. At any time, you should probably know or have handy:

- *A form of photo identification, such as a driver's license or state ID* (or other form of photo ID). Honestly, you'll want this wherever you go in the world, not just to doctors' offices or when you call to make a new appointment. Your driver's license or state ID can help identify you in an emergency and allow you access to adult spaces like clubs or bars, or you might need it if you get pulled over while driving. Don't leave home without it; Doug Blecher of Autism Personal Coach recommends that you keep a government-issued photo ID in your wallet or purse at all times.

- *Your health insurance card (if applicable) that has your group number, policyholder, and other information about payment and benefits.* Usually when you make an appointment at a doctor's office for the first time or go to a hospital in the US, they care about how you are going to pay for the visit or hospital stay. Providing this information also allows you to know what coverage you have and how much it might cost you to go to the doctor. If you do not have insurance, you might want to save money in an emergency fund or savings (more on that under "Financially Supporting Yourself") to pay for sudden, unexpected expenses like doctors' appointments or hospitalizations. (This doesn't apply to the UK.)

- *Know where your nearest local hospital is.* In the event of an emergency, you should know where your local hospital and urgent care centers (A&E) are. You should also have a plan of how you would get to a hospital: would you drive (if it is safe), take a rideshare, or have a family member or friend take you? Make sure to figure that out before an emergency pops up, especially if it is time-sensitive. If it is a true medical emergency, call 911 (999 in the UK) or your country's nationwide emergency number equivalent, and an ambulance will take you there.

- *A list of all medications you are taking or have taken.* This is helpful so a doctor has a clearer picture of your medical history. If you know why you stopped taking any of those medications (either due to treatment, allergies, or side effects), this may also help a doctor in coming up with the best treatment plan for you.

- *A copy of your medical records or chart.* In case there is something you aren't remembering (it's really hard to keep track of every vaccine you've ever had, or every medication you might have ever taken), a copy of your chart can help. Typically, other doctors have this on file or can provide it for your new doctor. Having access to your medical records is helpful for new doctors or if you are ever involved in an accident or even a lawsuit relating to an injury.

Medications and vaccinations

Any time a doctor has ever recommended medication, the biggest thing that happens to me is they will prescribe or recommend something without really explaining much about what it does or why it's being prescribed. I've gone to a doctor for an injury in my shoulder and walked out with a prescription for a wrist brace before! Needless to say, I did not fill the prescription. Always ask what you are being prescribed and why—it'll definitely help avoid funny situations like this before you have to go somewhere else to pick up your prescription.

The "in-house pharmacy" of emergency supplies

My dad is a pharmacist, so I have always grown up knowing to have emergency stuff around the house or wherever I lived in case I ever got sick. I like to have certain over-the-counter medications or treatments in a box or medicine cabinet no matter where I live, just in case I have allergies, headaches, or a cold. Feeling sick and having to go to a pharmacy or grocery store is not fun, but neither is suffering without treatment. Thanks to my dad, I have always known what to keep in my house in case of any mysterious symptoms, sicknesses, or major inconveniences. In your medicine cabinet or in-house pharmacy, you should have the following:

- *Band-aids (plasters).* You never know when you or someone you know will get cuts or scrapes or have a blister on their foot. I actually keep band-aids in my purse because sometimes new shoes might hurt me or when I am out with friends or co-workers, someone gets cut and then I look like a hero for having band-aids or something to help stop the bleeding or to cover the wound. It has helped my social life more times than I feel comfortable admitting—so, at the very least, having some emergency supplies at home or on your person can come in handy.

- *Q-tips (cotton buds).* You might use Q-tips for makeup

removal or to clean your ears; avoid using plastic ones, though.

- *Cotton balls.*

- *Rubbing alcohol.* This can prevent infections from cuts and scrapes, and can be used to treat acne, or to disinfect tick bites and certain surfaces in your house. It's an overall good thing to have.

- *Sunscreen and aloe vera.* You might not need these if you live in a cold climate, but if it is hot outside or you are easily sunburned, sunscreen can prevent sunburn, and aloe vera eases the pain and healing process of sunburn.

- *Cold medicine.* Colds and allergies are kind of the worst, and having a quick way to get rid of symptoms and to feel better will give you peace of mind if it's in your house before you get sick.

- *Ibuprofen.* You would be shocked how often headache medicine comes in handy. And in my experience, when you need it most, you usually don't have it—and no one wants to go to the grocery store or pharmacy with their head pounding.

- *Allergy medication.* Like many folks, I have seasonal allergies, so being able to relieve the pressure in my nose and congestion is a lifesaver. If you or someone you live with doesn't have allergies, you can skip this.

- *Icy-Hot®, or some other pain reliever cream.* Getting older means your body might act in new and not such welcome ways, or maybe you're also like me and you're kinda clumsy and might fall or bump into things every once in a while. If you don't want to take pills but want some quick relief for bumps, knotted shoulders, or muscle pain, over-the-counter pain reliever cream can help. Beware, though—sometimes they smell funky.

- *Any prescriptions you are currently taking.* Obviously, you want to have those in your house and remember to take them as directed. You will also want to pick up and call in refills as necessary (discussed next).

Picking up prescribed medication

Your doctor will likely call the medicine into your pharmacy, so you can pick it up the same day as your appointment or at a later date. Depending on your preferences and the pharmacy, they will call or text you when your medication is ready for pickup. When you go to pick up your prescription, you will have an opportunity to talk with the pharmacist filling it, and it might be helpful to ask questions about side effects, how and when to take it, or anything related to health and safety concerns surrounding the medication. Also, see how many pills are within the pickup so you know when you might need a refill, or who to get in touch with to rewrite the prescription for you.

To refill your prescription, make sure you have the information to call the pharmacy that you picked up from the first time (you can always call them and ask to transfer to another pharmacy that's closer to you or suits your needs better)—what your prescription is, your name and date of birth, who your physician is. The pharmacist will tell you when you can come by to pick up your refill. Don't wait until you are on your last pill; for refills, err on the side of caution—call it in when you have about two weeks' supply left in case of any emergency or if you are traveling so you have medication on hand in case something goes wrong or there are delays at the pharmacy.

Remembering to take medication and scheduling injections

Some days, I can barely remember to eat three meals a day. My executive functioning system occasionally fails and misses cues, so for some autistic folks, being vigilant about taking medication every day may be difficult. To help with this, be sure to keep the medication in a safe place to integrate into your routine each day. For critical tasks like this, I like to set a phone reminder or alarm that goes off and makes a noise at the same time each day, so I am held accountable. If you are on medication that requires an injection or administration at a doctor's office, schedule those appointments far enough in advance that you won't forget!

Each year, I also know that getting a flu shot is important. I've always had rough times with the flu, and I could not afford to miss weeks of school or work. Each October, I make a point to get a flu shot; often, your local drugstore, community health organization, or other retailer (I've gotten a flu shot at my grocery store's pharmacy and at a retail store/supermarket before) will offer them at low cost or incentivize you with a gift card to get a flu vaccine in October–November or thereabouts. Usually I set a reminder at the beginning of the fall season, or my family reminds me because they get theirs around the same time.

Tracking side effects

Sometimes, medication and treatments do things to our bodies that are not in line with what they are supposed to do or cause unintended consequences. These side effects can be major or minor, but if you are a nervous person who collects information and decides to look up all side effects on the internet, you might be convinced that you're dying. Chances are, you aren't, but it might be worth talking to your doctor about them. Keeping a list of side effects and medication can also make talking to your doctor easier and help you weigh the pros and cons of whether or not to continue a specific course of treatment. Your medication might be responsible for some of the symptoms you have on your other lists or for other weird stuff going on with your body like hair loss or something you might not have thought was medical in nature.

COPING WITH MASSIVE LIFE CHANGES AND STRESSFUL EVENTS

Regular stress and anxiety are part of everyday living, but major life events within and beyond our control can make for unique challenges. For instance, I began writing this book during the COVID-19 pandemic. In the span of less than a few months, I left a full-time job, started my own business, was traveling almost every other week as part of my business, saw the cancellations and postponements roll in because of public health concerns, and then moved home with my parents in order to quarantine (and after those few months, I moved back to my apartment again). Needless to say, I experienced a lot of life changes and stress all at once and with a lot of different factors—I went through changes in employment, routine, income, and living situation, uncertainty in the world with a public health emergency, and an upcoming political election with massive implications for the lives of those around me. This perfect storm of change can be difficult to cope with for a neurotypical person, but for my autistic self, the feelings were overwhelming. I was grieving the loss of opportunities I was really excited about, like giving a TEDx talk and speaking at the United Nations. I was worried I would not see my friends again for a long time. I felt helpless because moving back home affected my routines and what I am used to, as well as ensuring I did not do any activities that would put my family at risk of contracting the virus, and I still had work left to do. To say I felt stressed, anxious, and disappointed or upset to some extent is an understatement.

Losing loved ones: holding space for grief

I am a fairly upbeat, positive person, and writing about death is not something I ever thought I would do, although since entering adulthood I have lost two grandparents and my family dog of 14 years. I have felt different about each loss, sometimes feeling overcome with emotion, sometimes able to continue business as usual. The latter unnerved me—am I the stereotypical autistic person who lacks empathy (although we know autistic people are highly empathetic humans)? At other times, I was numb and unable to do anything, often explaining to friends and colleagues that I felt out of touch or was distracted by the immeasurable feeling of loss.

Wondering if perhaps autistic people experience grief differently, I reached out to Karla Helbert, a therapist, bereaved mother, and the author of *Finding Your Own Way to Grieve: A Creative Activity Workbook for Kids and Teens on the Autism Spectrum*. She tells me there is no "one size fits all" to grief, meaning we each experience different emotions over time related to grief. Some of us may have trauma, or feel indifferent, angry, or sad.

Karla tells me that for her autistic clients, grief is a major stressor. Like many stressful things for autistic and neurotypical people alike, the way our bodies and brains react to stress will be amplified. Our nervous systems may be aroused. For autistic people, we might have heightened sensory experiences or be more prone to overloads, meltdowns, and shutdowns because of the stress caused by our grief of losing a loved one. Common autistic and neurodivergent traits, like certain cognitive challenges, attention issues, executive functioning issues, and even a lack of eye contact, can all be magnified during grief. But most people don't know that these heightened experiences or what they are going through are results of grief and loss, because, as Karla explains, "our culture does not deal with grief at all, so we don't know we're going to feel these things."

Karla also reassured me that my feelings about reacting incorrectly or performing grief were normal for most people. It can be confusing for those around us, but "inappropriate affect" is a response to grief and trauma, hence there are people who laugh at funerals.

When I asked for recommendations to best help autistic people, Karla had a few:

- *Find a therapist who understands both grief and autism.* Karla especially recommends this in light of the heightened sensory experiences and cognitive demands on our brains. Also, if you are seeking a diagnosis or are undiagnosed, a more experienced therapist might be able to help you get formally assessed for autism. Karla has had clients whose losses led to a diagnosis because of the severity and onset of new sensory issues, or because the trauma compounded autistic traits.

- *Join a support group.* Everyone in a support group may have different stories related to loss, and some of the members might also be neurotypical. While you might have unique backgrounds, the shared experience of grief and of losing someone close to you is one that can validate your emotions, too. Karla shares that grieving people struggle a lot with people not understanding their experiences—whether it's family members, friends, colleagues, or even professionals and therapists who simply write off the person's experiences as being depressed.

- *Have a strong support system.* This is especially crucial for those who have traumatic grief, meaning they do not adjust well following a death. Karla says the people who do best have strong support systems: they have family members and friends they can rely on, understanding people around them, good mental healthcare, a good therapist, or a combination of these. She considers people who are "help-seeking" people to be the ones who manage and accept their emotions best—so don't be afraid to talk to somebody or find others going through a similar life event to rely on, too.

- *Practice self-care.* While self-care is discussed more throughout this book, Karla recommends knowing how to take care of yourself as a strong grieving skill. This includes being a strong self-advocate, so you know how to express what it is you need right now. It is okay to remember to take care of yourself in whatever way you can to calm down during these highly stressful, difficult times, and do whatever you may need in order to decompress and relax. Don't forget to eat and drink, and try to get enough sleep if possible, too.

When someone else is grieving

There is no right way to react to someone else's grief. If someone you know experiences the loss of a parent or a pet, even letting them know you are there for them can be more than enough. If you are aware of funeral arrangements or are expected to go to a memorial service, make sure you dress conservatively and pay your respects in accordance with the family's wishes: some families, religions, and cultures do not want you to bring flowers, but would rather you make a donation in the deceased's name. If you are unable to attend, consider sending a sympathy card expressing that you are sorry for the loss so that your friend or whoever is grieving knows you are thinking about them during a difficult time.

Karla tells me it is frustrating when people assume a person will simply get over losing a loved one, a pet, or a friend in a matter of days or weeks, or make a comment like "You're still not over it?" There are many things you can do to show you care: you could call or text someone who is grieving, offer to bring them food, or partake in a favorite shared activity together. But don't feel offended if they turn down your offer; maybe they prefer to be alone, or don't feel up to having visitors or socializing right now.

While grief is seen as taboo in many cultures and can be difficult to talk about, there is one clear reminder: as long as you love another person, you'll grieve. You might not have that intense grief constantly, as when the loss is still fresh, but it can be reactivated for years with things that remind you of a loved one, like birthdays, holidays, or memories you shared.

Quality time with things you love

As autistic people, we are often viewed as inspirational figures of a cluster of symptoms and traits, and our special interests and things we love are often pathologized as part of autism. But these are things that bring us joy and deserve our attention. This is something that came full circle for me very recently in conversations with Becca Lory Hector, the autistic host of the *Infodump Files* podcast, where she and her co-host talk to autistic people about the things they love most (when I spoke to Becca, we had a lengthy discussion about why potatoes are the perfect food and which French fry reigns supreme). Our interests are varied and intense. Some, like trains, are deeply embedded in autistic culture. Others are more nuanced and unique to us.

Unfortunately, neurotypicals are not always as understanding or rise to the level of interest Becca takes in her guests on the Infodump Files. Sometimes, we can't merely "infodump" and share everything we know about the things we care about with another person because they aren't interested or don't understand that our willingness to talk and educate is a sign of love and caring.

But no matter what your special interests or intense hobbies are, or what neurotypicals think of them, they bring you an immense comfort and happiness. Set aside time to spend with these interests, especially after long and stressful events. Do not just give up on the things you love because of masking or a plea for acceptance from neurotypicals. These interests and passions make you the wonderful autistic human you are. Carving out time each day to do something that makes you happy or that you enjoy will help balance your mental health.

Friends and family should also recognize the joy we get from our special interests, even at holidays and other occasions. Attempting to get us to branch out doesn't go nearly as well as allowing us to "infodump" or giving us a gift related to the things we already know we love.

Healthy Habits

Our bodies react to the way we treat them: when we make good decisions with the amount of sleep we get, what we eat, exercise, and take care of our minds, we perform better.

ESTABLISHING ROUTINES

I feel like establishing routines is the crux of this book—how to set specific routines for specific aspects of independent living and self-advocacy skills—alongside knowing when to ask for help as an interdependent community member. But, as part of having healthy habits, having a daily routine to take care of yourself is crucial to your wellbeing. While we autistic folk thrive on sameness and routine because it brings us comfort and the ability to focus, having a routine for the mundane stuff in life (not just our special interests or how we browse the internet or do a specific task) is what ultimately keeps our worlds in orbit.

To establish a healthy, daily routine, think of the stuff you do every day and would like to do consistently. In this section of the book and throughout I address some of the things you can think about. If it helps you to write out a schedule of sorts, go for it:

- *When to wake up and when to go to bed (try to be consistent).* Do you need to set reminders and alarms to let you know to rest your eyes before bedtime and stay away from screens, or do you need a certain sound to wake you each morning at the same time? Also, keep in mind your routine and bedtime and that when you wake up might be different on weekends, holidays, or days off from work or school, or other adult commitments.

- *When to eat.* It is easier said than done to eat three meals a day or to eat enough nutritious food to keep your body going.

- *When to take a shower.* You have to bathe every day—morning or evening, more than likely.

- *When you need to be at work or some other place for the majority of the day (i.e., classes if you're still in school).* Usually this accounts for a big block of your day, but if you are in school, each day of the week might look a bit different.

- *When you might set aside time to exercise or have "me time" for relaxing or hobbies.* It's important to take care of yourself, and sometimes explicitly writing this down or scheduling it can bring calm.

- *Social activities/regular meetings or appointments.* If you meet with a support group, therapist, social club, or something every single week at the same time, that's also part of your routine. If you are like me and call your mom the minute you get home from work to talk about how your day went, this is also part of your routine.

ACTUAL BUBBLE BATHS: PERSONAL HYGIENE ROUTINES

Personal hygiene can be difficult for autistic people not because we prefer to be seen as disheveled or unkempt, or do not want to be clean. If you're out of the house, you probably don't have your parents to nag you to be a clean, hygienic person (although if you do live at home, heed their advice on this one—and if you need the assistance of a caregiver, ask). Chances are, since you set your own schedule and also have responsibilities, there is nobody telling you when to take a shower, comb your hair, or brush your teeth. And people will notice if you have bad hygiene.

Hygiene skills involve fine motor skills, executive functioning, and sensory processing—for instance, autistic teens and adults might not consistently wash their hands or brush their teeth because of the amount of little steps the tasks need to be broken down into, like getting to the sink, finding the soap or toothpaste, turning on the water, etc. all going through our head rather than just automatically doing the thing neurotypicals do, which is not really thinking through or worrying about staying on task, or there is also the sensation of the bristles on a brush or the warm water on our hands. With this in mind, personal hygiene is still something we need to upkeep as part of our independent living skills that keep us healthy, and so other people don't avoid us because of how we look or smell or think we are gross. Like most things, the beginning of good hygiene is to set a routine.

Bathing

Thankfully, a lot of these routines probably won't have changed since you were a child or teenager. You will still want to regularly take baths and showers, use soap and body wash, and deodorant or antiperspirant (especially if you sweat a lot). Depending on your schedule, you might either shower first thing in the morning and so everything is super-fresh feeling for work and wakes you up, or shower right before bed to help unwind and destress a bit. Be sure to build this into your routine every single day to avoid smelling bad and making your adult social life even worse—as my mom once told me, no one is kind enough to tell you that you have body odor; people just avoid you instead.

Hair care

One of the biggest personal hygiene tasks that is somehow all-encompassing for me is my hair. I did not know how to use a hair dryer (which saves me so much time and also makes the texture of my hair so much more bearable from a sensory perspective) until I was in my late teens, and I am still trying to figure out the science of using all the different styling brushes. I own a straightener, but famously ended up using it in college once to iron my then-boyfriend's dress shirt because at the time neither of us owned a clothes iron, and we assumed that hair straighteners worked similarly. I am not gifted at beauty-related stuff, but some parts of hair care and beauty beyond the hair dryer and straightener are part of appearing neat and clean, and taking care of yourself.

Washing your hair with shampoo and conditioner helps keep your hair and scalp healthy. Depending on your hair type, you might have to do this every day. If you have natural hair, you may need to upkeep your hair with different oils and moisturizing products.

Haircuts

Regardless of whether you dye your hair or do anything special to it, chances are you need to regularly have your hair cut or visit a salon to keep it neater looking, out of your face, or to keep your hair healthy to avoid split ends. While haircuts can be a nightmare for autistic people, remember that there are stories on the news related to kind folks cutting autistic kids' hair for free or finding a way to do it while we remain calm. There are some ways we can make the experience a little easier.

You might choose to cut your own hair or have a friend do it at home to avoid the crowds or sensory-related and accessibility challenges of a salon or barber shop. Just know that if you are not a professional, there might be a chance your hair doesn't turn out the way you want it, or you may need the expertise of a stylist. Traditional haircuts can be a sensory minefield, between the talking, sounds of hair dryers, electric razors and other styling tools, sitting with wet hair, waiting and being expected to sit still while color is processing or while someone is cutting your hair—it can be a lot to deal with. To help ease the burden, see if your local area has sensory-friendly businesses, or businesses that work with organizations like KultureCity, or try to schedule appointments at off-hours (1 like to go early in the morning, to avoid the rush). That way, there are smaller crowds, fewer tools whirring around, and you might be able to walk around or stim more while waiting.

Stylists have told me that we should get our hair cut somewhere between every six weeks and every four months, depending on your look and desires. 1 try to do a trim more often than a full cut since 1 have bangs (a fringe) that easily cover my face and get in my way if 1 don't regularly upkeep them, but each to their own.

Shaving and body hair

Some hygienic and grooming choices are a matter of personal preference, like shaving. Not everyone chooses to shave their arms, legs, or face because of gender expression, personal preference, or cultural reasons. That's okay. Some people think it is cleaner, prevents odor, or is sensory-friendly to be clean-shaven because skin is smoother. Others feel better with body hair. This is entirely your choice. If you are removing body hair, though, make sure it is maintained through grooming, safe practices like clean razors and shaving cream, wax, and also washing yourself regularly to prevent infections.

You can also make appointments at professional salons or with cosmetologists for hair removal. I personally will not mess with my eyebrows myself (I like them shaped), so I make an appointment every few weeks to have them threaded or waxed, and I'll maintain them as best I can when something grows in the middle since I do not want to have a unibrow in between appointments.

CLOTHES

I know, we like wearing the same things and stuff that is comfortable. I hate wool sweaters with a fiery passion because they itch and feel absolutely horrible against my skin, and sometimes I have to cut the tags out of skirts or pants (trousers) because they also itch. I am also someone who is very passionate about fashion (it's one of my varied interests that I know a lot about).

Shopping for clothes is one of those things that as young adults we have to do while also keeping our needs and societal expectations in mind. Our sense of style evolves as we get older, but there are essentials every person should have.

No matter what, you should own comfortable shoes (sneakers, especially if you walk a lot or also exercise), a few dress shirts or blouses, jeans, slacks, or a skirt, and, of course, essentials like undergarments and socks (I recommend overstocking on these—there is nothing worse than running out of clean socks and underwear before laundry day). For a formal or black-tie occasion, like a gala or a wedding, you should have a suit and tie or a nice cocktail dress or ball gown (I think you can get more mileage out of a cocktail dress, though, since you can adapt it to other situations). And, of course, you need fun clothes like t-shirts, tank tops, shorts, and whatever you wear around the house or out with friends.

Also, depending on what you do for work or if you're going to events, you might need to have clothes for every type of dress code. Some of the common dress codes for work or social events are "casual," "professional," or "black tie." There might also be themes, but for the big ones, there are some ways to navigate and figure out what's best to own.

I find "casual" to be the hardest to dress for since everyone has very varied interpretations of what they might wear. In some places, this might be jeans, and in others, it might be shorts or skirts. I think professional attire is more straightfor- ward and conservative—those nice dress shirts with bottoms, a well-fitting dress with a blazer, and dress shoes. And "black tie" is the simplest of them all—a nice suit or a dress, the nicest of the nice stuff you own.

If you're looking for style suggestions, I recommend check- ing out influencers, magazines, or people you admire. If you want to get the look without spending an arm and a leg, you can always shop sustainably through second-hand shops or online marketplaces; otherwise, there are lots of retailers and stores you can order from or shop at.

NO-STRESS REST: SLEEP ISSUES, INSOMNIA, AND FEELING RECHARGED

Ah, sleep. The elusive thing that is supposed to come to us each night in order for us to feel rested and recharged. I feel like I haven't had a consistent sleep schedule since high school, back when I used to get up at 6 am each weekday without fail and fall asleep by 11 pm after homework and studying. Since then, a barrage of other things has got in my way. I'd stay up all night talking to someone I cared about. I'd wake up in the middle of the night worried I was failing in school or something had happened. I'd sleep in late because I could, or because I had had a rough night. Maybe I would take a nap in between classes. When I began working, I would wake up at the same time every day, but bedtime was always a little bit more up in the air, although I'd try to be asleep before midnight (sometimes I worked really late because I had fewer distractions at night), but I wouldn't sleep through the night. Part of adulthood, as far as I know, involves regularly feeling tired.

Regularly feeling tired is not uncommon for autistic people. In an article for *Spectrum*, Hannah Furfaro documented different studies and perspectives on how and why this is the case. Autistic people struggle with sleep and insomnia, often taking longer to fall asleep and having difficulties staying asleep; we also cycle through the stages of sleep differently compared with neurotypicals (Furfaro 2020). Our sleep difficulties can be tied to co-occurring conditions or medications we're taking; sleep difficulties might be associated with depression and anxiety, or stimulants to treat co-occurring ADHD might be keeping us awake (Furfaro 2020). Or it's just straight-up genetics or a difference in our neurologies that researchers haven't quite found the answers to. Either way, sleep is something we struggle with more than the neurotypicals, and it matters.

Lack of quality sleep has consequences for autistics. That tiredness exacerbates social difficulties like making friends or interacting with others and leads to more meltdowns and less ability to go with the flow (Gholipour 2017). It makes concentrating more difficult. In other words, we probably appear more autistic when we are sleep-deprived because it impacts our mental health and capacities to mask and socialize, and our worn-down systems are on overdrive interpreting the world around us, thus making us more prone to anxiety and meltdowns.

If this is the case, how do we get better sleep—or at least, consistently try to?

- *Go to bed at the same time each night.* I know, this seems like a comforting routine, but sometimes life gets in the way. To keep you on track, have an accountability buddy, set an alarm, or try to have a nice little bedtime routine right before you want to go to sleep to get you ready for some shut-eye.

- *Limit screen time before bed.* For me, this is probably the hardest thing to do since I tend to play games on my phone, watch TV, or check social media before bedtime. Find a time before bed to call it quits on technology, and use that time to take a shower, brush your teeth, put on your pajamas—do whatever it is that'll help you know it's bedtime.

- *Exercise during the day.* I'd stay asleep during the night on days I exercised and feel more rested because my body also needed the time to recover from working out.

- *Avoid or limit caffeine.* I am not a coffee drinker, but for those of you who are reliant on caffeine from coffee or energy drinks, these might indirectly be keeping you awake or interfering with your sleep patterns, even if you're using them to stay awake and alert. It can be a vicious cycle. Cutting caffeine completely can be really difficult to do and lead to withdrawal. One recommended way to limit caffeine without ditching it completely is to stop drinking it past 2 pm or at some point in the afternoon.

If your sleep problems persist, perhaps get a sleep study or see a doctor for prescription sleeping pills. Sometimes, a study or brain scan can help answer questions to solve the problem of lack of sleep.

FOOD AND MEALTIMES

Food is one of those complicated things when you're autistic. For me, food is not just how the texture hits my teeth and tongue, but it is also the colors, the shapes, the tastes, and the smells. There's also the executive functioning aspect of it: purchasing food, preparing and cooking food, keeping track of what might be priorities to eat, making plans with others—it can just be overwhelming.

And finally—food is a lynchpin in social interactions. Most outings with friends and colleagues revolve around food, whether it is meeting at a restaurant, grabbing a drink or dessert, going to a potluck dinner party, or cooking a meal for you and your partner.

With so much to think about in terms of food, eating, and mealtimes, I spoke with Dr Elizabeth Shea, a clinical psychologist and co-author of *Food Refusal and Avoidant Eating in Children, including those with Autism Spectrum Conditions.*

Sticking to a schedule

As someone who struggles with executive functioning or gets so hyper-focused on things, it can be difficult to stick to a schedule for meals and snacks. I'll lose track of time and forget to eat when I am busy or get really wrapped up in something.

Sometimes, as Dr Shea pointed out to me, autistic people also struggle with recognizing when they're hungry or even full. This is due to what I have also learned is called "interoception," where we miss bodily cues like hunger or thirst, or if we're hot or cold. Because our bodies might not recognize whether or not we are hungry or thirsty, sticking to a routine and eating around the same time each day can help cut out the guesswork and wondering "Did I eat enough?" or "Did I forget to eat today?"

Limited diet and picky eating

One of the most visibly autistic struggles of mine has been picky eating. When I was a toddler, I would eat anything—to my parents' shock, I truly enjoyed butternut squash—but since passing that stage, food has been problematic for me.

You might not be a picky eater per se, but enjoy "samefoods," as the autistic community puts it: having the same thing to eat, presented the same way, brings joy and comfort. Or you might be on a limited diet because of an underlying medical condition or allergies. You might need to eat food that is gluten-free or casein-free.

If you are a picky eater or on a limited diet, you might have some extra things to think about in terms of health and food in social settings.

- *Check restaurant menus ahead of time.* Anytime someone suggests where we are going out to meet and eat socially, I check the online menus if possible. The menus or at least some of the most highly recommended things to eat are either in a place's press coverage or review sites like TripAdvisor, or the establishment has a readable version or PDF of their menu online.

  I like to know what to order so it fits my needs. For others, it might also help in avoiding any anxiety associated with choosing under pressure or communicating with the waitstaff. If you don't see anything you would possibly order because of a limited diet or lack of samefoods, you might gently suggest meeting up somewhere else (for neurotypicals, I found a good script is "Hey, that sounds cool, but I'm really craving something else. Would you like to go here instead?").

  Dr Shea agreed, telling me that checking menus can ease anxiety. She also said you can do something similar if you're going to a friend's house for a meal by asking what they will be serving. "It's okay to ask what food someone is serving at their home," she assured me, adding that asking is not, in fact, rude or poor etiquette. Neither is telling your host what you will have to eat based on the options being offered.

- *Consider bringing a snack with you or eating beforehand.* As one of history's pickiest eaters, this strategy has possibly saved my life. Eating as a social activity is kind of strange, and sometimes people are not accommodating in the settings in which they choose to gather or meet for a meal. If you feel like joining everyone, bring a snack with you (if appropriate), or eat something before meeting up with others; when you get to the restaurant or other place, order some water or another drink. Usually, people don't pay too much attention to this afterwards, and will be more mindful of accommodating your dietary needs in the future.

- *Know how your body will react if you deviate.* This is for my friends who are lactose-intolerant or can only eat gluten-free food or who have other sensitivities and allergies. If you decide to eat gluten or dairy and rebel against either your allergies or sensitivities, what will happen? Will you have a severe allergic reaction that is potentially deadly (e.g., peanut allergy)? If so, you probably need to be extremely careful and mindful about what you eat and the ingredients in meals to stay safe. If you are doing a limited diet for health concerns, consult with your doctor or other medical professional.

  For me, my body reacts funky with ice cream, although ice cream is one of my favorite foods. I sometimes have to weigh up if I am okay with feeling sluggish or sick from it, or otherwise eat it in moderation.

Trying new foods

Fun fact: I probably try a new food every five years. Trying new foods make me anxious because I have to think about the sensory profile or deviating from a routine. Discovering pizza in my early teen years was truly a game-changer since it meant no more going to birthday parties and celebrations just for the cake (birthday parties were too much for me socially as a kid, but I would always stay because of the promise of any flavor of cake). While the pizza parties seemed to be few and far between in my teen years, my relatively new discovery was a social mainstay of my college and law school years. In the college dorms, my fellow dorm resident friends and I ordered pizza at least twice a week. A lot of club meetings I went to in law school served pizza for lunch, and it meant I was socially able to eat during the group meetings. But trying new things fills me with a sense of curiosity along with a sense of anxiety. I want to try new things, but I'm also scared. It is definitely an internal struggle for me.

Dr Shea tells me that this struggle is not uncommon for autistic adults. While samefoods and eating according to a routine often bring us comfort, we might want to venture beyond our comfort zone and try new foods too. Dr Shea emphasizes that it's important we feel comfortable doing so. As we get older, we naturally might want to try new foods because we either get bored with what we typically eat or are in more social situations where diversifying our personal menus might be necessary to reduce stigma or judgment, or we have a desire to fit in.

To decide what to try, sometimes it's as simple as beginning with foods you like, Dr Shea tells me, and then branching out from there with new flavors, brands, packaging, or shapes.

For example, one of my favorite foods is French fries. If I want to venture beyond this, I might want to experiment with fries from different manufacturers or restaurants (I don't insist my fries be from the same place), or I might go for shoestring fries, curly fries, or wedge fries instead. These might be less intimidating to sample or be adventurous with because I already know I like traditional fast food fries. If I am feeling adventurous, I might want to try something similar to fries, like potato chips, because they are also potato-based products (for the record, I do like potato chips; they remind me a lot of fries, although they are baked and the ridges and feel of them are very different).

Dr Shea recommends doing "taste trials." They are kind of like experiments to see if you like something or not. To try something new, you don't want to be anxious about it, so try a relaxation technique. Don't do a taste trial because you are under peer pressure from friends or family around you; it's up to you to determine what, when, and where you want to try to expand your palate. Ideally, you'll also do these away from mealtimes. I get that—not liking the meal I'm trying for the first time in a social situation would make me very nervous because I wouldn't want to tell someone who had cooked it for me that I didn't like it, or feel uncomfortable at a restaurant surrounded by colleagues, friends, or family I am going out to eat with.

For "taste trials," Dr Shea says you should try a very small amount of the new food, rate the food on a scale of 1 (really don't like it) to 10 (really love it), and repeat this a few times so your brain can register if you like the food. If you consistently don't like it, don't force yourself to try to love it. Move on to a new food.

Ultimately, you are in control of what you eat. Whether or not you choose to branch out or feel ready to try new foods is totally up to you!

Making healthy eating decisions

This is not a diet book, and I am not commenting on anyone's weight related to the food they eat. All I am doing is trying to encourage you to make choices that nourish and honor your body's needs and that keep you healthy. Making good choices can leave you feeling more alert and energetic, and also limit other health problems like heart disease, diabetes, or breathing difficulties. Some of our autistic friends also have co-occurring gastrointestinal challenges, so they have to be mindful of what they eat to avoid inflammation or further complications. In other words, make decisions around your individual wants and needs, to keep your body and brain working and able to help you crush life!

To help you make a few decisions and not feel stressed about it, my biggest recommendation is to *enjoy things in moderation*. Some of the biggest struggles we have are with interoception and realizing when we are hungry or full, and then we might just keep eating too much and not recognize our body's natural cues. Or maybe we just crave the same "junk food" because it makes us happy, even though it means we get bad stomach aches. If you are a limited diet person, or "healthier" options are inaccessible or unappealing to you, try to moderate the portion size or frequency of what you eat. One of my favorite things in the world is pizza. While I can't eat it every day, I will not inhale the entire large pizza by myself because then I get really sick, sluggish, or unable to sleep.

Cooking

I am by no means a great cook. I am, however, particularly skilled at reheating pizza and chicken, and following instructions for frozen food. For some people, cooking is cheaper, fun, and an alternative to ordering in, eating pre-packaged food, or going to restaurants. I am lucky my mom still cooks for me and I'll freeze and reheat the food she makes me. Learning to cook is something on my bucket list. If you want to learn, you can ask a friend or family member to show you, or take a cooking class (this is also a fun way to possibly meet people and learn a new skill).

For those (like me) who want to be better in the kitchen, it begins with owning equipment and cookware. Personally, I own an array of pots and pans, a toaster oven, and a blender. My apartment already has a microwave and an oven.

Every great cook, baker, or chef I have talked to in my personal life says that cooking is a lot of trial and error or being able to follow directions. You'll want to get some comprehensive cookbooks or find some great recipes online or that are passed down through relatives. Any ingredients you may need you should prepare for in advance and pick up when you go to the grocery store as part of your errands.

Cooking can be a cumbersome task for many reasons. For some, it could be the sensory experiences of mixing different textures and how everything feels to the touch, working with our hands and having not so wonderful motor skills, or struggles with executive functioning and the organizational steps involved in timing things in ovens, when people get home, recognizing our own hunger, and how long each food preparation step might take. It might take me under a minute to heat something up in the microwave, but when I last helped my mom bake a cheesecake, it took several minutes to combine the ingredients, a half hour in the oven, and then it had to chill in the fridge for about four hours. If I was making a cheesecake for dessert with dinner, I'd have to plan it out much farther in advance than I would reheating something already made.

In an attempt to figure out my aversion to cooking (or why I seem to shy away from it), speaking to Dr Shea was enlightening. She recommended autistic people begin learning how to cook or getting used to it with something psychologists call "graded exposure"—start with a simple step and then work your way up to the hard thing, at your own pace. That way, we will not become too stressed, or overloaded, or the task won't become too difficult.

The first step in this exposure is some motivation. Seems easier said than done, but some motivators to start learning how to cook (or do it independently) are that we probably shouldn't eat random products and rely on other people to prepare meals for us (whether they are relatives, housemates, or chefs in restaurants) all the time. Sometimes we have other motivators, like wanting to fit in with other independent-seeming adults, preparing a nice surprise or gesture for a romantic partner, or we are taking care of other people like family members.

If the number of steps and processes in cooking seem like a lot, Dr Shea recommends truly starting small. You could start by watching other people, like friends and family, do the cooking. She told me autistic people learning to cook can "begin pouring, stirring, weighing, measuring ingredients" so you are practicing interacting with food and ingredients without directly touching them—basically, less sensory exposure right off the bat. If you're feeling braver, you can begin other preparation steps like slicing or chopping things. Certain ingredients are easier to interact with because they might not be sticky, wet, or slimy. Slicing a loaf of bread is a lot different than slicing meats in terms of smell, texture, and other sensory aspects. If touching things that seem tricky feels like a lot, you can always wear gloves to avoid direct contact and getting too close (this might also be safer when dealing with certain raw ingredients).

The social aspect of food: eating with others

Come to think of it, almost all social activities somehow involve food. Going to hang out with friends? You might be going to a restaurant as a group or eating a meal at their house. Visiting family? They more than likely will want to cook for you or take you to a restaurant. A romantic date? Probably involves some kind of food. Major occasions like birthdays and weddings? They definitely involve food (and probably cake too).

But going out to eat, or eating with others, poses social questions other than what is on the menu. Dr Shea mentions some of the social rules we might not even think about—where do we sit at a table with a group? It might be easier to sit next to someone than across from them because you might not have to make as much eye contact. But, as Dr Shea pointed out to me, the person next to you might have their food too close to you, it might smell bad, or your food might disgust another person—you might accidentally offend the vegan next to you if you order meat.

There are also the questions of social norms and manners. Do you wait until everyone is served their food before eating? I'm never quite sure of the answer to this—sometimes, if you wait too long, the food might get cold, or your host absolutely insists you begin eating without them.

Also, who pays the bill is an eternal question at restaurants: in a social outing with friends, each person typically pays their own way, but the rules may be different if you are on a date or with family members. So is how much to tip the waitstaff (20 percent is usually fair and generous for service in the US, in my opinion, but tipping customs vary worldwide).

GET MOVING! EXERCISE AND STAYING ACTIVE

My physical fitness journey and life has been interesting, to say the least. I began riding horses in early childhood when I was about four or five for hippotherapy, helping with my motor skills and sensory input. It turned out I was a gifted equestrian and began participating in local horse shows (I have a collection of ribbons and trophies to show for it!) up until I had a career-ending injury at age six during a practice ride—I busted my right arm. Following my horse days, I spent many, many years dreading physical education and gym class: I was one of the slowest runners and was always picked last for team activities and sports, seemingly for both social purposes and for my lack of athletic prowess. Of course, this means I ventured back into the desire to join a sports team when I was a high school freshman (Year 10 in the UK), deciding that I would join the rowing team. I enthusiastically signed up for the summer rowing team training camp, and after some intense workouts on land on the first morning, we were finally ready to climb into the eight-person boats and spend our first hot Florida afternoon on the water. The oar felt heavy and I was very sweaty. After a few minutes on the water, we returned to the dock. I climbed out of the boat, felt dizzy, and fainted before reaching the boathouse. Passing out after the heat on the first day of rowing camp sealed my fate in two ways: (1) I would not complete the next few weeks of rowing camp, and (2) I would not try out for the rowing team. I would avoid athletics altogether if I could help it, hanging my head for another year of being picked last in gym class.

Once in a while, I would go to the campus gym to walk on the treadmill or use the elliptical machine to avoid spending time with my freshman roommate, but I didn't dare revisit athletics or join an intramural sport (recreational sports leagues and teams) in college or law school. That changed when I was 22, when I was right about to enter my final year of law school. I felt burned out that summer, so a friend invited me to go work out with her. We went to the campus gym together, where I was overwhelmed by the harsh fluorescent lights, squeaking sneakers shuffling around, and intimidating-looking equipment.

Determined to try again, I took a day off from work, and following my friend's suggestion, I went to an indoor cycling class. For 45 minutes, the outside world disappeared. I immediately fell in love with the dark room, the coordinated dance moves to thumping bass and loud music, and the corresponding light show. It felt like a safe version of going out with a group to a bar or club—instead of alcohol, there was sweat. Instead of a dance floor, there was someone in the front of the room telling the crowd to lean to the left or right and what to do next with our bodies while also saying we were strong and looked confident. It felt euphoric, and, if anything, the choreography felt like synchronized stimming—our bodies moving to the beat of the music all together for 45 minutes.

I went to indoor cycling classes at least twice a week as a treat or something to look forward to for well over a year. I made a few friends along the way, too; the instructors who saw my progress were also people who eventually congratulated me and shouted me out during class when I graduated law school and when I passed the bar exam. I would eventually switch it up with different classes—all I knew is I needed the accountability of someone telling me what to do so I wouldn't injure myself, and knowing I was supposed to show up somewhere at a specific time.

Your mileage may vary, but your fitness journey—or commitment to moving your body—might look a little different. It's not about what activity you do, whether it's dance, cycling, weightlifting, running or walking, or playing a team sport; it's about just moving your body.

The benefits of exercise and movement

At the very least, the Centers for Disease Control and Prevention recommends moderate physical activity to help with sleep, reduce the risk of depression and anxiety (movement can also alleviate symptoms of depression and anxiety), reduce the risk of certain chronic health conditions, improve thinking, learning and cognition, and other health benefits (CDC n.d.). Weight management or weight loss can also be a benefit, if that is one of your personal health and exercise goals.

If you don't know where to get started or want to feel some of the benefits, just try to go outside and take a short walk.

Exercise is a celebration of what your body can do, not a punishment

I learned this from friends who are in recovery from eating disorders. Viewing movement as a blessing and an activity rather than as a chore or punishment for what you eat makes the task more enjoyable. I am not exercising because I ate too many fries. I move my body because it wants to move. It was designed to do these things, and when I am active, I feel happier and more energetic, get more rest at night, and can focus with the adrenaline coursing through me afterwards. I also feel challenged, like I am growing into someone who is mentally and physically stronger.

To make exercise and movement feel more like a celebration or less of a dreadful thing, experiment until you find something you like or feel that you can easily put into your routine. Maybe you need a coach or trainer to tell you what to do (no shame, I like having someone tell me how to do things), or you have a specific goal in mind. Think about how much time you'd like to realistically sink into exercising each day or week, and use that as a starting point.

For a goal, I like to ask what folks are hoping to achieve. Maybe they want to fit into an old pair of pants (trousers) again, or feel confident with who they see in the mirror, run a marathon, see changes in their bodies, or establish better habits. Your goals are personal. I recommend writing them down to keep yourself accountable because if moving does begin to feel like a chore, you'll remember why you started or are continuing, and what you are working towards at the same time. It's an extra, needed boost of motivation and confidence.

Making physical fitness spaces accessible

For autistic people, one of the biggest barriers to joining a gym, fitness club, class, or team can be the sensory or social aspects.

For me, a lot of gyms are overwhelming because of those harsh fluorescent lights I once experienced in college campus gyms, or the smaller studios might play the music too loud and it feels overly competitive, and then I feel self-conscious.

Mikhaela Ackerman, an autistic yoga instructor who also blogs at Edge of the Playground, wants the yoga sessions she leads to be welcoming and safe environments for neurodiverse groups. To make her classes more accommodating, she uses softer lighting, and verbal and nonverbal cues, and provides weighted blankets or sandbags. She also avoids using strong-smelling incense or essential oils for those with smell-based sensory processing differences (or allergies, for that matter).

If you're concerned about accessibility in a smaller group setting, try to talk to the instructor beforehand. They typically want to get to know their students and clients. See if there is a less busy time on the schedule or a more relaxing vibe under the class description—a slower-paced yoga class or beginner level class might have fewer distractions, fewer people in the room, and more individual guidance.

DRUGS AND ALCOHOL USE AND ADDICTION

It is easy to hear the old adages about avoiding drugs and alcohol and not to succumb to peer pressure. Yet, for various reasons, people on the autism spectrum might have issues with dependency on drugs and alcohol, amounting to a substance use disorder. There is a difference between drinking occasionally or socially and having a substance use issue like addiction to alcohol or drugs.

Addiction is a substance use disorder and a potentially co-occurring disability. You may have a genetic predisposition to it because of autism or family history. Researchers in Sweden found that autistic people are more than twice as likely to become addicted to drugs or alcohol than their neurotypical peers

(Butwicka *et al.* 2017). Addiction and autism have biological and psychological features in common, according to those studying the two disabilities. There are similarities in the way addicts and autistics use repetitive behaviors to cope emotionally, as well as in their impulsivity and compulsions. The two conditions affect some of the same brain regions and involve some of the same genes (Szalavitz 2017).

Autistic people might take up drinking alcohol or abusing prescription drugs in order to ease social anxiety or in an attempt to fit in. Others might have turned to misusing substances in order to cope with the sensory environment. The consequences, however, can be drastic—loss of social life, termination from a job, dependency on the substances, financial hardships, or a turn towards the illegal.

If you do choose to drink, do it in moderation and know your limits. If you are taking prescription drugs, do not use anything that is not prescribed by your doctor, follow the dosage spelled out for you, and use the medications as directed. Know how these substances affect your coordination, judgment, socialization, and if you are safe—for example, that you are aware of the consequences of drinking and driving (you can be arrested and/or possibly hurt someone). If you do not feel comfortable drinking socially, it's no one's right to demand to know why, and you can just politely decline. Your ability to socialize or be included should not hinge on whether you are consuming alcohol or incorrectly using narcotics.

If you are seeking help for addiction, know that there is no "one size fits all" approach. Group therapy or a 12-step program might be particularly difficult for autistic people because of the social dynamics, but other options like residential treatment or working with mental health professionals individually may be helpful. And, of course, if you are struggling with mental health as the root cause of substance use, do not hesitate to seek help.

Socializing

AN "ADULT" SOCIAL LIFE

Having a social life as an adult feels like an entirely different animal compared with when I was in school or college. I don't just meet people because I am thrown into a living situation with a bunch of my fellow students in the same building or we are taking the same classes. The people I went to college and law school with are now scattered across the state, country, and in some cases, the world. Our lives have taken us in different directions, so our friendships might not have endured the test of time. Also, I see far fewer people in a law firm situation than I would milling around university campuses. Needless to say, my social life as an adult has changed drastically from when I was living at home as a high school student and when I was in postsecondary education settings.

When I reflect on who my friends are in my mid-twenties, the picture looks a little bit different. I have my work friends, who aren't all people from my office. I have my lifelong friends I have known since childhood or who are family friends. I have a collection of people I work with and am friendly with. I also have friends I've connected with in some way or another, and friends who come and go.

Making friends as an adult and meeting new people

Making new friends is probably one of the hardest things I've had to learn how to do once I left school and realized all of the "forever" friends I would meet during college and law school were not, in fact, "forever" friends. Out of the closest friends I had during college, I only regularly speak to one. My closest friends during law school have moved out of the area and we rarely talk, mostly on birthdays and holidays now. Sure, staying in touch is something we do—but we have grown apart as we are physically apart, also making new friends, or as we enter new chapters of our life with home ownership or marriage. Friend breakups are one of those things that don't get enough attention, and if you and your friends grow apart as life changes happen, it's okay—it's not your fault. How did I make new friends once I started my job and entered a new phase of life? Here's what I learned:

- *Put yourself out there.* What does this even mean when neurotypicals say it? Turns out, "putting yourself out there" means giving yourself opportunities to meet people. This is how I made most of my current friends. I posted on social media about things that interested me and made friends on autistic Twitter. Mutual friends can help, too: a friend of mine asked if they could give my information to an aspiring lawyer (who, after a first meeting, quickly became one of my closest friends); sometimes, a mutual friend might just know who you'd get along with that they know. I also joined professional associations for lawyers, often linking up with others in the field around similar interests who didn't work inside my office.

    You also have to be a little bit aggressive, as much as that sounds kind of difficult. Don't be afraid to invite someone to an activity like a movie or a game night, or out dancing or shopping. Follow up with people. Take an interest, get to know them, and work at it. Friendship is a two-way street, but sometimes, the only way to make new friends is to be pushy and to make the first move.

- *Make old friends new again.* This also means you can re-connect with old friends you might have lost touch with! Take that initiative, send that text or Facebook friend request to the person as long as you did not part on bad terms. I've reconnected this way with high school friends or friends from childhood even for just a quick catch-up. I wouldn't recommend it with former romantic partners, though, since you never know what their intentions may be. You can't make old friends; just make old friendships stronger. And you never know, your old friends might introduce you to their friends, and thus you are also making new friends. Renewing old friendships is also a lot easier since you already know each other. It's about putting yourself out there and taking that step to reignite the connection.

- *Join a social group.* This is a good way to meet people with similar interests. Try to join a club or organization revolving around a special interest or hobby. There are community groups and activities for everyone, ranging from groups of gamers, to casual pickup sports leagues, workout classes, or movie nights. If you are looking for ideas, check the app MeetUp where social groups are always looking for new members. You can also join a social group for autistic adults in order to make new friends and meet people with similar experiences and in-terests, if that appeals to you. If there are no social groups near you, you can always start your own and begin to befriend the people who show up and join. Most people are shockingly more alone than social media makes them appear to be, so they want to meet new folks as well.

- *Don't be afraid to use the internet.* Some of my friends came from Twitter and social networking. This way, you can meet people who share your favorite interests or who you can play games with—often without having to leave home. Friends of mine have remained friendly with people they met on dating apps but did not end up dating. But, of course, as discussed earlier and in terms of dating, your safety online is paramount. There are also other apps that foster connections and friendships and the rules still apply.

Staying in touch and keeping friends

Keeping in touch with people is part of growing and maintaining friendships. Depending on how close your friendships and relationships are, you might talk to some people every day, once a week, once a month, or more randomly.

Certain check-ins and contacts I have are non-negotiable and I will put them in my calendar. I always make sure to have written down the birthdays of close friends and family members. That way, I know to send a birthday card (and, depending on our relationship, a gift) as well as call or text them. It's a small way to show I remember and care, and it goes a long way.

Depending on how important someone is to you, make sure to figure out if it isn't natural how often you would like to talk to them. For some people I will send a check-in or a "thinking of you" type message once a month, just to catch up. Others I'll reach out to when I feel like it, or if there is a major life event. Sometimes they will reach out more often than me, and I respond when I feel up to it or think I can be a good, attentive friend or want to hang out with them. When I was having a hard time, one of my autistic friends checked on me exactly a week later just to see how I was. I found it touching, and he admitted he had placed it on his calendar after our last conversation—I found that to be a cool piece of advice, and I never would've guessed otherwise. We all have the capacity to care and show one another we care, and needing a little reminder or push in the right direction does not make us worse as friends.

I have a lot of acquaintances and friends, and sometimes knowing whose messages and phone calls to prioritize can be overwhelming. To keep people who call and text me organized, I use a specific system of emojis next to a person's name to signal to me who is a priority in my life. It also helps when I see notifications and can quickly make snap decisions as to how urgent and important something may be. I mark my closest friends with a fruit emoji because fruits are sweet and I value their friendship. For acquaintances and folks I would like to be better friends with, I use a seedling emoji, signaling that this is a relationship I would like to grow—these are what I call "seedling friends," new friends, or people I see often but would like to be better friends with. I use different emojis for work-related colleagues, so I know the correspondence is business-related. It also helps me regularly take stock of who I need to follow up with and stay in touch with—sometimes, I owe my fruit people a "Hi, how are you?" and the emojis help me keep track or realize who I need to check in with.

KEY TAKEAWAY

- Find a way to determine which friendships and relationships mean the most to you. How often do you talk to, or want to communicate with, these folks?

Social networking and social media—a hobby or a tool?

One of the nice things about social media is that it has helped me make friends—with people I haven't met in person, mutual friends, or colleagues I don't get to spend too much time with. Facebook has been an invaluable tool for me to meet and connect with lawyer colleagues across the state and country I've worked with and been to events with, but never got to hang out together with. People also feel safer messaging me with private things, like sharing they have loved ones who are autistic—which they might not have felt comfortable doing in a face-to-face setting. I have also used tools like LinkedIn to connect with leaders in my industry I don't know in order to ask questions, network, or somehow learn more.

Social media is also a way to stay abreast of what is happening in the world, sharing pop culture, memes, and news articles. You might also use social networking to find community on places like Discord for gamers or to be part of the very robust autistic community.

Privacy and internet safety on social media are always paramount. You might be using social media like Facebook, Twitter, and Instagram to connect with real-life family, friends, colleagues, and classmates. It is a way to stay in touch through the messaging features or to just casually know what is going on in people's lives. Or you might be trying to make new friends through shared interests and communities.

Validity of online friendships

Probably one of the most hurtful things I have heard recently is that "internet friends are not real friends." While I understand the risks and privacy concerns associated with connecting with people you might not know in person online, people we are connected with through the internet are also real people. For young people, they often make friends they might not have otherwise made online, and are reliant on technology to stay in touch (UK Safer Internet Centre 2018).

Some of my closest friends from the autistic community are people I have yet to meet in person, but we are connected through in-person friends or colleagues. They are a lot like long-distance friendships because we don't live in the same cities. We call and text regularly and share what goes on in our lives. These friendships are absolutely real and can make you feel connected. Just make sure who you are talking to is who they say they are, and you are not getting into anything illegal like sexually explicit relationships with people under the age of 18, or stalking them.

DATING 101

One of the most fascinating things to me about being in my mid-twenties is realizing I've seen people go from meeting their romantic partner for their first date to now being engaged, anticipating a wedding. Some people I know are just having fun, simply meeting people when they feel it suits their schedule. Dating in your adult life can be because you're looking for a life partner, exploring your sexuality, having fun, meeting new people, or sharing new experiences with others. Whatever your reason for dating, it is important to be safe, to maintain boundaries and healthy relationships, and possibly even find love and companionship.

For many autistic people, finding someone to share our lives with is a goal and something to strive for. Sometimes it is something our families fear for us: that we won't find someone who loves us for who we are and who we love back. I have never been the kind of person who writes or talks about dating and relationships, but I have learned a few things over the years.

The first is that autistic people do find love. I've been in several relationships with guys I can say I loved and who loved me back. I have many autistic friends who are in serious relationships, are casually dating, or are in long-term partnerships or marriages. It continually fills me with hope. There are also autistics educating other autistics on sex and relationship boundaries like Amy Gravino, an autism and sexuality advocate.

The second is that love is not just with other autistic or disabled people. While docuseries like Netflix's *Love on the Spectrum* only show autistic people gearing up to go on dates with other autistic people (or autistic relationships), we also have sparks with neurotypicals. There is a myth that we have to be with or settle for our own kind; while autistic partners can have wonderful relationships, they are not our only options. All autistic people can have healthy, supportive, kind, and loving relationships and marriages with anyone regardless if they share a similar neurology. I particularly think of my friend Zack Budryk, a reporter at *The Hill* who is autistic and co-hosts the *Stim4Stim* podcast about autism and relationships, and his wife, Raychel, who is non-autistic. Zack and Raychel's relationship always manages to bring a smile to my face because of how much they support and love one another.

While I can't say for certain what my specific romantic future holds, I do know this: I've been fortunate to give and receive love. And since autistic people aren't all doomed to have loveless lives spent in our parents' basements until the end of time either, I get to give a few tips on how to meet potential partners, stay safe, and answer the eternal question of how to talk about autism to people you are dating.

Meeting people

The beauty of the modern world is that you can meet potential romantic partners pretty much anywhere. My friend Zack met his wife Raychel in college through a student organization. One of my neurotypical friends met her now-fiancé on a dating app (although we all went to school together, they knew of each other but had never spoken before matching with each other); I remember her anxiously texting me before their first date. Since societal structures and norms have evolved and changed, the most effective and common ways people meet have also changed. Typically, couples meet through mutual friends, religious organizations, community groups and activities, or even at work (as much as office romance is frowned upon). However, the emergence of the internet has changed all that with dating websites and services taking the world by storm, along with the surging popularity of dating apps.

Dating websites and apps

A lot of singles—and autistics—feel that they have a better shot at meeting their potential romantic partners on dating websites and apps. Meeting online is the most popular way couples meet today (Rosenfeld, Thomas, and Hausen 2019).

Dating websites and apps are also a way that autistics exploring their sexuality or recognizing they are queer might feel safer meeting potential partners, especially if they are not yet out offline. The internet offers some refuge and community building for people of different sexual orientations, although like most things online, privacy is a concern. It also offers the ease of text-based communication. Some popular dating apps are Tinder, Bumble, and Hinge. Some of the most popular dating websites are OkCupid, eHarmony, and Match. Other apps and websites may be geared towards people with diverse religious backgrounds or sexual orientations.

Safety

One of the most important aspects of a relationship is feeling safe—emotionally and physically. When entering the dating world, physical safety and preventing domestic violence, abuse, and sexual assault are always at the forefront.

It is not okay for someone to violate your boundaries, emotionally or physically. If a conversation is going somewhere you feel is inappropriate, makes you uncomfortable, or you are being coerced into doing something you don't want to do, end the interaction, report the person, and block or un-match them. No online dating platform tolerates abuse and harassment.

Meeting someone new for the first time

If you are meeting someone new for the first time (either taking a conversation offline or through a blind date), be sure to keep safety at the forefront. Dating apps and websites take safety seriously for their users, and after reviewing some of their tips, I wanted to expand on some of them in order to make you feel safer—even if you're just meeting a mutual friend you've never met before.

- *Don't meet up right away.* While it is fun to talk to a new person and see if there's chemistry between you, exchange messages first or maybe video or audio chat first (you can do this without giving too much personal information). See if this is a situation that you feel comfortable with.

- *Avoid giving out too much personal information.* Even in this day and age, where everyone searches for one another on social media, try to avoid giving out too much personal information too early, especially if this is someone you met through the internet or a dating app.

You don't want strangers having your phone number or knowing where you live. To try to minimize some of the risk (if you want to move the conversation on from a dating app), you can get a second phone number through an app like Burner or Google Voice to keep your main number private, or you could set up a new email address just for dating websites and apps to keep anything too steamy out of your main inbox and also to protect your privacy. You can give out your regular information if you feel comfortable with this person later on down the line, maybe after a few weeks or dates.

If you don't know how much personal information exists about you on the internet, try searching your name online and see what shows up. Maybe some photos show up or your social media handles and posts are public. As a general internet safety precaution, make your profiles private to avoid your data being accessed by people you don't know (or by people you might not want to see your profiles), including random people on dating websites and apps (if you're on them), job recruiters, college and graduate school admissions offices, and colleagues.

I have a large digital footprint chock full of social media and photos, so to help separate personal and professional work and lives, I have a separate email account for personal correspondence, and a Google Voice phone number, and am also very judicious about what pictures and information I share online.

- *Meet for the first time in a public place.* Ideally, this would be during the daytime to eliminate some of the fear associated with going out at night. Perhaps meet for coffee or at a park or something low key to ease your nerves. Most people prefer night dates like dinner. If you are feeling creative, some ideas if you are suggesting or planning a date are to go to a movie, a restaurant, or an activity together (one of the most fun dates I ever went on was to a painting class—I didn't even plan that), doing something touristy in your city or town, volunteering, or going to a museum.

As much as it may seem sweet to offer to pick up the other person for your date or to have them pick you up, meet at the public place you agree on in case the date goes bad, so you are in control of the situation. You wouldn't want a complete stranger knowing where you live right away—what makes a first date any different? You also don't want to be reliant on them to get home if things don't go well.

- *Be sure to let someone know where you are going and who you are going with.* Tell someone who you are with, the location and time you're supposed to be going somewhere, and text them at some point before the date is over to let them know you're safe (a great way to do this without seeming rude is to excuse yourself to go to the bathroom, and then fire off that text). Another idea is to have a code word with your friend or other person around, so if the date is not going well or you feel uncomfortable, you can say the word to them and they will call you or help get you out of a situation (you can then give your date an excuse like "I am so sorry, my best friend just broke up with her boyfriend, I need to be there for her") to rescue you or give you a reason to leave, pronto.

- *Pick an activity with a set start and end time.* As much as I strongly dislike movie dates unless it is someone I know and have been dating for a long time, I find them incredibly predictable as first dates—we meet maybe an hour before the movie to talk or grab something to eat, and then we might go our separate ways after the movie. It is easy to let people know what you're doing, where you are, and how long you'll be there—and you can easily update them if your plans change after the movie. Dates that are less flexible and fluid also mean you can get out quickly if you feel uncomfortable. Also, it can be kind of overwhelming to be spending too much time with someone you just met!

Sexual assault

For women and other gender minorities, the fear of sexual assault or exploitation is particularly valid and real. People with intellectual and developmental disabilities are seven times more likely to be victims of sexual assault compared with nondisabled populations (Shapiro 2018).

Disclosing autism to a potential or current romantic partner

How do you date when you have a disability? Disclosure in the workplace (discussed later in the book) is one thing, but disclosing in dating is a whole other thing. I sought to answer this question by writing an article about it for *GQ*. When writing and researching for *GQ*, my goal was to speak to disabled and neurodivergent people about disclosure, not the neurotypical people who reacted to disclosure. I was lucky enough to interview several autistic and disabled folks. People shared that depending on their disability, self-worth, and level of trust with a potential partner, all determined when and how they shared something like if they were autistic.

While I am openly autistic in my personal and professional life, dating has always been another arena. I have had potential partners treat me differently or stop talking to me after disclosure, and I have also been fortunate enough to have very supportive dates and partners over the years. No matter how nice someone has been to me, I always dread talking about autism for the first time with someone new in a romantic setting.

When to disclose is kind of a mystery to me. Some folks recommend disclosing up front, like on a first date or before agreeing to go on a first date—that way, it weeds out the ableist neurotypicals who have a negative bias towards autistic people.

What I learned from speaking to others for *GQ* is there were a few different approaches for disclosing:

- *Wait until autism comes up naturally.* In my life, autism comes up naturally pretty early on. If I haven't met someone in person yet, anyone worth their salt will Google my name out of curiosity, or to make sure they feel safe and know who they are talking to. Even if not, it still creeps into conversation early on—I might mention I was on television before, or when I am asked about work, I might answer that while I am a lawyer, I am also a public speaker or that I am an expert on neurodiversity in law. When I'm asked about work, it almost immediately prompts a follow-up question like "What do you speak about?" or "Neurodiversity and the law? What's that?" and depending on the situation, I will mention that I am autistic. If it is a first meeting or date or early on, someone might just brush off that disclosure, or we will have an extended conversation about it because they ask follow-up questions. Sometimes the conversation evolves over time; other times, it feels very formal depending on how much exposure the other person has had to autism.

  With another autistic partner, it might be far more natural to disclose early on and share more aspects of autistic identity. Explaining stimming to a neurotypical may feel different than bonding with an autistic match over shared stims or figuring out how autism impacts each of you individually. You may also feel more at ease communicating with someone who is autistic as well because you can both engage in autistic culture and leave behind some of the neurotypical social and dating conventions (if you so choose)!

- *Use a prepared statement.* A prepared statement helps you have the autism conversation in a positive manner, while also maintaining and respecting your boundaries. In your statement or script, you might plan to explain how autism affects you—if you're giving it early on in a courtship or dating, it might be better to downplay disability and highlight the strengths to ensure you get that first date or next date. Deciding on when in a relationship or courtship you want to disclose might depend on the depths of how much you share about your autistic identity. You might scare off a potential match if you share too much too soon, or they may be incredibly understanding. Make sure your statement feels true to you!

  To write out or plan a prepared statement, think about what you might want someone to know about how your body and brain operate, especially if it may impact where you go on dates because of sensory issues or special interests. You might just say, "Before we go out further, there is something you should know. It's a thing I explain to everyone I meet—I'm autistic. It means my brain works a little differently, I'm really passionate about the things that interest me, and sometimes I struggle socially and in loud and crowded places. Hopefully that's not a deal breaker for us." You don't have to give too many details early on, but just enough that you are able to get your autism out in the open and possibly weed out people who won't accept you for who you are.

- *Allow the conversation to deepen over time.* Whether or not you mention you are autistic for the first time in a dating profile, in the messaging phase, or on one of your earliest dates, chances are you will continue to have more intense conversations about autism and how it affects your life as time goes on. Saying you are autistic is not a one-time thing; chances are, you can't cover every aspect of your diagnosis or autistic identity and culture in one conversation (I certainly can't). Maybe you won't be telling a neurotypical partner the ins and outs of every sensory experience or challenge you have, or educating them on disability rights history, but you might begin to share more about your personal experiences and advocate for your needs as your relationship develops.

While the conversation begins pretty naturally for me, how much I go into depth about my autism will evolve based on my comfort level and situations. Disclosure is an ongoing, evolving conversation. Sometimes disclosure on a subtler level can be admitting I need clear communication or want to avoid a restaurant that doesn't have chicken dishes or pizza on the menu because of my food aversions and desire to eat the same things. On a deeper level, sometimes a date and I might talk about social justice and the struggles of being openly autistic in specific settings.

I first learned about the evolution of disclosure and the natural growth of autism conversations when I went to a basketball game with my then-boyfriend in college and felt a sensory overload coming on because of the squeaking of the shoes (he and I left early, and he took me home once I had calmed down), or when we eventually went to a concert and I struggled with the noise. A few days after the concert, we talked about what sensory overloads feel like and tried to map out how to avoid triggering them in the future. It was a tender moment, and an organic, deeper conversation I had with someone I had known for several years at that point—definitely not something I would have wanted to discuss straightaway after telling someone I was autistic for the first time.

Managing rejection and heartbreak

Chances are, you will have a lot of "one and done" dates—or you'll decide not to meet in person after all. You might not have any chemistry with the person or want to pursue a relationship or friendship with a new person, or they might not want to pursue a relationship with you. It could be for any reason, and your feelings (and theirs) are valid.

Sometimes rejection can be blunt, like someone saying they are not attracted to the other person, or it can be gentler like, "I had fun, but I don't think this will work out." Others have more confusing behavior, like saying they are constantly busy when asked about seeing them again, or they will stop responding to calls and messages altogether (this is known as "ghosting," and whether you are ghosted or doing the ghosting, it usually means the ghosting person is afraid or too immature to honestly discuss their feelings; it is not your fault).

If you are rejecting someone, communicate respectfully and clearly about boundaries and that you aren't interested in dating anymore. Try not to hurt their feelings too much—you can let them down by saying you're busy until they take the hint, or you can say that you enjoyed spending time with them but don't want to pursue a serious relationship. This is easier if both parties don't want the same things—if someone wants a purely sexual relationship and you want a serious romantic one, you can say that you aren't looking for something casual and nicely wish them good luck finding what they are looking for.

If someone rejects or breaks up with you, it is okay to feel hurt. Consider talking to a family member, close friend, or therapist to sort out your feelings. Like many young people, I have experienced heartbreak (either as someone who ended a relationship or mutually ending one). For me, self-care, talking to others, and spending time with my favorite special interests or throwing myself deeper into a school or work project would help me get used to being single again. You do not have to start the dating process over again until you feel ready, safe, and emotionally available and open to meeting new people once more.

Whatever you do, do not engage in harmful behaviors towards your former partner or the person you were dating. It is not appropriate to pursue someone after a rejection or heartbreak. Harassing them, showing up at their home or work unannounced, sending gifts, or continually asking someone on dates after they reject you can make the other person feel unsafe and can also lead to legal consequences for actions like stalking. If you do want to talk to the person again, be respectful and ask in order not to violate any boundaries or make someone uncomfortable.

Meeting your partner's family

You are in a healthy, loving relationship and your significant other wants you to meet their parents—or you want to introduce them to yours. Depending on your situation, this step might be incredibly important and happen after months or years, or if your partner lives with their family, it might be more of a casual formality.

Meeting family can be a high-stakes event. Most families only want the best for their children. Your family will have opinions about your partner, good or bad. Similarly, your partner's family will have opinions about you, so it's best to make the best impression possible.

How to make a good impression
and what to talk about

Since I am not a parent who has ever had to meet her children's romantic partners, I am not best equipped to tell you what works. I have met boyfriends' parents and family members before, and I learned they like me if I take an interest in them, listen to what they have to say, am polite, and am also able to demonstrate that I care about my partner who happens to be their beloved son/brother/nephew/relative. How exactly do you show you care? And what did my parents think whenever they'd meet whoever I was dating? To help answer these questions, I spoke to my mom about how to make a good impression on someone else's family.

My mom recommends when you meet a partner's family (or their parents) for the first time, you bring a gift to their home. Your partner probably has some ideas of what their parents like or would appreciate. If there is no guidance, a bottle of wine, a dessert or some type of food, or a bouquet of flowers typically go over well and are regularly appreciated. It shows that you care, want to make a good impression, and are well mannered, polite, and also respect your partner and their family.

Family members and parents always want to know the person they love is also loved and cared for. Try to highlight your partner and the nice things they have done for you or your relationship. My parents specifically mentioned that they appreciate knowing that someone has my back, and there might have been a small thing that someone did for me I may not have told my parents about before. Family want to see how you make each other happy.

Things to avoid doing

When I attempted to rush (join) a sorority in college, an older student gave me the following advice on which topics to avoid talking about under any circumstances, because no matter what, they left a bad impression. Those topics were "booze, boys, and bank." I like to apply the "booze, boys, and bank" rule when talking to new people generally, especially important ones. You might have these conversations solely between you and an established partner if they are within the boundaries of your relationship, but they are not okay to bring up with your partner's family the first time you all meet.

Under "booze," the wisdom was to avoid talking about partying and excessive alcohol use—you don't want anyone to perceive you as irresponsible, reckless and careless, or immature. If you suffer from alcoholism or another addiction (and are in recovery, relapsed, or are sober), it might not be the strongest foot to lead on; it is highly personal information that might cause unnecessary judgment on a first meeting, no matter how brave you are for managing and thriving right now.

"Boys," at least when I was taught this in the sorority context, meant not talking about boyfriends, hookups, and dates. While your relationship may be with someone of the same sex or a different gender identity, when meeting your partner's parents or family, it still applies. Do not bring up your past relationships and ex-partners/dates, your sex life with your partner, or anything too intimate. Talking about people you used to date (or wanted to date) is not appropriate with your partner's family—they'll be left wondering why you're with your current partner and not the old flame you can't stop wistfully talking about.

"Bank"—while financial literacy and having discussions about your finances with your partner is likely going to happen within your relationship (money troubles and disagreements are one of the most common reasons people break up or file for divorce), it is not appropriate to bring up your salary, your partner's money issues, or to ask your partner's family about money. Just avoid it altogether—anything your partner may have told you about their family's finances should stay in strict confidence.

While not part of the "booze, boys, and bank" rule, I also actively avoid talking about politics. Political engagement is crucial and important (as discussed under "Making My Mark on the World: Self-Advocacy"), but it might not always be worth mentioning on a first meeting. As much as I am opinionated on current events and politics, I know it can easily lead to arguments with people I don't know very well, or them making a snap judgment about me based on my beliefs, so I try to steer clear unless I'm actively invited into that conversation and feel comfortable. I also avoid anything too philosophical about religion, knowing full well that people can be judgmental and difficult; if you are invited or having a first-time meeting for a religious holiday, I recommend keeping the tone light and celebratory (or solemn, if it's a serious, reflecting occasion).

Ruler of My Own Domain: Having a Home

Moving into my first apartment was possibly one of the most nerve-wracking and exciting few months of my life. I was 20 years old and about to embark on a new chapter because I had enrolled at the University of Miami for law school. Since I would be moving over 50 miles away, I had to get a new apartment close to the campus. I was so unbelievably giddy working with my family to gather everything together; I had lived at home the year I graduated from college and right before starting school, so I was starting from scratch on getting everything together. My new place was a one-bedroom, one-bathroom empty box with a kitchen, living room, bathroom, and bedroom—small, but absolutely perfect for my new life. Over the course of several weeks, we shopped for and ordered furniture to be delivered to my new place, picking out sofas and chairs, a kitchen table, a bed, and nightstands. My mom stocked my kitchen with pots and pans, silverware and plates, and, of course, filled my pantry, fridge, and freezer with food. I hung artwork on my walls. My dad made sure my appliances worked and helped me set up lamps and my TV, and made sure the hot water, air conditioner, and washer/dryer were in tiptop shape. Over the course of about a week, I had my very own home completely set up, down to fresh white sheets on my bed, and I was thrilled. No dorm room could compare, and neither could my beloved childhood bedroom (which has many of the nostalgic trappings of childhood, like my doll collection).

Then I realized, as beautiful as my new home was, I had to take care of it.

HOUSEHOLD MAINTENANCE: CLEANING, AVOIDING STARING AT OLD PHOTOS, AND EXECUTIVE FUNCTIONING

Taking care of your home requires time and effort. You might need the help of others for repairs, maintenance, housekeeping, setting a routine, cooking, or any of the many tasks to keep your home functioning. And, of course...there are the more cumbersome tasks, like cleaning, laundry, avoiding getting bugs, going grocery shopping... I'm not going to lie: chores are probably the most dreadful thing in the world. Good news: chances are, if you live alone, no one will yell at you to do them. Bad news: if you keep putting them off, your living space will probably end up dirty, smelly, and disheveled, and if you have a roommate, they will absolutely hate you for it.

Mail and packages

In today's world, we get a lot of mail, right? Whether it's advertisements, magazines, bills, or the random, exciting thing we ordered online, things come in the mail a lot. Try to make a habit of checking your mailbox once each afternoon or evening as part of your routine when you get home. Sort through and discard things that are not important and open the things that are urgent and/or important.

If you are expecting anything important or want to know what mail and deliveries to expect, you can sign up online with all the major delivery carriers for their version of a delivery monitor. USPS Informed Delivery® sends daily emails letting you know what mail is coming to your address—that way, I know if I am expecting payments, bank statements, postcards from friends, packages sent via Priority Mail, or even just junk mail. It saves me the occasional trip to the mailbox. I am also signed up for FedEx Delivery Manager and UPS MyChoice®, so I can either schedule packages to arrive when I am home to avoid them getting stolen, or I know to be home in case someone has to be present to give an authorized signature accepting the package.

Since there is always a chance you are sending snail mail either to pay bills (more on that later), stay in touch with friends, or send out packages, you should have stamps and envelopes to hand. You can buy stamps online, at your local post office, convenience store or grocery store; the same goes for envelopes. Write your return address in the top left corner of the envelope, put the stamp on the top right, and write the address of the person you're sending it to in the center of the envelope (it never fails to amaze me how many neurotypical young people don't know this since they think everything can and must be done online).

I don't have mailing boxes since they take up a lot of space, but in the US the post office provides free mailing boxes if you order them online, or you can recycle the ones from past things you had delivered.

Cleaning

Cleaning my apartment is quite possibly the absolute peak of my executive functioning challenges. Every single Sunday, without fail, I would wake up and plan to use the day to catch up on household chores like cleaning and laundry. I would take the cleaning supplies out from the cabinet under the sink, as well as have my vacuum and mop ready to go. By the time I had the leather cleaner, countertop cleaner, bleach, rags and paper towels, and other products ready to go, I would feel infinitely overwhelmed. Or I would tell myself to start small and just do the major surfaces like the floors and bathroom. I would wash down and bleach my shower and use bathroom cleaners and disinfectants for the toilet too, and then I would get distracted somehow. And even if I managed to get my apartment clean for the day (what I figured should take no more than about 90 minutes somehow took me hours on end), I would always feel like I had missed a surface or some of the baseboards (kickboards), which I would save for when I did a deeper clean every few months.

You should probably own or have access to the following:

- a vacuum

- a mop

- a glass and surface cleaner for windows and mirrors; i also have a leather cleaner for my leather couch

- gloves

- cloths and towels

- sponges

- a bucket (for water and soap while you mop, or also to store your cleaning supplies in).

A (semi-foolproof) cleaning plan

My biggest barrier to cleaning is distraction, so here is the best way I have found to avoid getting too distracted: leave your phone charging in another room but leave the sound on in case of an emergency (I get distracted by wanting to check social media or texting people, so this helps me).

My first step always is vacuuming the floors. I also like to play music to make the vacuum seem less loud and startling to the senses. After the floors, I do surfaces, dusting, and details. Start in the room with the least amount of clutter or decor, since this is probably the place with the fewest likely distractions. For me, this is the bathroom area, so I always vacuum on the way to head there before I bleach and sanitize my floor, toilet, and shower. Then I wipe down the counter, mirror, and sink. There aren't a lot of decorations or things out on the counters like toothbrushes or the like, so the bathroom cleaning flies by compared with places like the bedroom, where I have more stuff. I purposely set more time aside for my bedroom since I do have things like old photos, cards, important papers on my desk, or other objects that might spark something or cause my mind to wander.

Doing the little things each day

To make cleaning less miserable, try to incorporate it into your routine each day. While that may sound even worse, it's actually pretty simple:

- *Try to put things away during the week as you use them.* This is probably the hardest task because of executive functioning, but the easiest because if you keep at it regularly, it can take less than five minutes a day. Somehow, things become a lot less overwhelming if you don't leave all of your clothes on top of a chair or a spot of honor on the floor. Put things away when you're done with them and don't let the clutter pile up. Put papers in folders or in your desk drawer. Try to keep surfaces clear when you aren't using them, so you don't get ridiculous amounts of dust. If you put stuff away, it's one less thing to do on cleaning day! Ha!

- *Do at least one smaller task each day, like vacuuming.* If I remember to do it, I vacuum my bedroom and bathroom every day—mostly because I shed like a cat and seeing strands of red hair on the floor most days is unsightly. I feel like I'm achieving more when it doesn't take me as long to do it each time thereafter. Some days I might just use the mop to upkeep the shine and eliminate dirt. I might also make my one daily task taking out the trash, doing the dishes, cleaning out a cabinet, anything that somehow makes me feel like I've accomplished something and makes the one day I set aside to do as many cleaning tasks as possible feel infinitely less overwhelming and much more doable.

- *Clean as you go.* Some tasks might be easier to do as you do things around the house. Did you cook a meal today? If so, make sure to wipe down the kitchen appliances and counter, brush the crumbs away, and do the dishes or other tasks. All of these little things add up, and not doing them can lead to a disaster later on.

- *If it's really too overwhelming, stick to high-traffic areas.* On days I feel cleaning is too much for me, or executive functioning is not allowing me to deep-clean my apartment, or I don't have as much time on a Sunday as I'd like to dedicate to making my house spotless, I will only clean the highest foot traffic areas. These are the parts of my living space I spend the most time in and tend to get the dirtiest. For me, those places are my bedroom, bathroom, and entryway (lots of marks from shoes from entering and leaving the house). It saves time and helps with upkeep. If I feel up to it later or on another day, I can then do the more secondary living spaces that get less time spent in them, like my kitchen and living room.

  One exception to this high-traffic strategy: get rid of anything that can bring bugs in or is just plain gross.

Seriously, don't let stuff keep piling up in your sink, and if you see mold in your bathroom, get rid of it ASAP.

- *If you need help, ask your family, roommate, or hire house-keeping help.* When I was in law school, my parents used to come and visit and help clean my apartment every other week. While I felt a little embarrassed that I needed the help because I thought I would be able to do it all by myself, my study schedule and other obligations, as well as executive functioning, often made this difficult. I was eternally grateful for their help, and it became my task to upkeep the job throughout the next two weeks.

If you have a roommate, try to figure out the best way to divvy up the tasks or ongoing maintenance—that way, the responsibilities are split in half. No matter what, your bedroom is your space, so it is your responsibility to remember to try to put dirty clothes in the laundry basket or clean clothes back in your closet or dresser—especially if you have guests coming.

Kitchen tasks: dishes and garbage

I might not be a great cook, so cleaning and taking care of my kitchen is not as high a priority for me. For your kitchen, the folks at Apartment Therapy recommend having dish soap (washing-up liquid) (a no-brainer), dish towels, and sponges (Coffey 2020).

I like to wash down my plates and silverware with dish soap and use a sponge before placing them in the dishwasher to get rid of any excess residue before it sticks and hardens on the dishes. Don't let the dishes pile up in the sink for days on end. It will create extra work for you, and the food residue might attract unwanted insect visitors. It is also unsightly and makes the day you decide to clean your entire house that much worse—and if you have housemates or a roommate, they might have different organizational habits and not want your stuff clogging up the sink you share together.

Spring cleaning: kitchen and pantry edition

Something I don't do every single week—but recommend you put on your calendar or consider this one of your cleaning or house maintenance tasks along with your roommate (possibly)—is going through the food in the fridge, freezer, and pantry for expired or stale food and related products (you should also do this with your medicine cabinet). Depending on the product, you might not want to have rancid leftovers in your fridge for weeks, or you might want to throw out expired yogurt. It is one of the easiest tasks to do, and also one to do at the same time as you make your grocery list since you'll know what you need and what you might not regularly use if you keep it to the point of expiration. Expired products can be dangerous for your health, or in the case of things like medication, be less potent and effective. I find this cleaning task weirdly fun and also disturbing since I realize we keep things way too long, and I also know what'll need to be replaced next time I go to the store.

Taking out the trash

You are probably going to want to take out the trash once a day so you don't have a stinky home or too much overflow in your garbage can (rubbish bin). Or you'll want to take it out multiple times when you do a big clean. You might want to buy garbage bags for your trash or you can re-use paper and plastic bags from grocery shopping or other stores (I do this because I have a relatively small trash can). Also, if you can, be a friend to the environment and recycle your paper, plastic, and glass. I like to use a cardboard box, usually left over from a package or mail delivery, to place my recyclables in each week or so—that way, I can also recycle the box at the end when I take it downstairs and don't have to bring it back up with me. If you have a roommate, you could set a schedule for recycling and trash and alternate which of you goes to the dumpster or recycling bins each week in order to share responsibilities.

Laundry

When I lived at home, my mom did laundry every single day. I never quite understood how three people generated enough stuff to wash each day, but I suppose between clothes, towels, kitchen towels, and bed linen, there were plenty of items to be washed and dried. But then I realize my mom did laundry every day so she didn't have to spend hours doing loads, especially delicate items or things that required a special wash. Thanks to her diligence and ownership of a high-tech-looking washer/dryer, I was pleasantly surprised when I first got to college and went to the dorm laundry room, put all my clothes in what I thought was the washing machine, and was confused as to why they were warm and soapy. Needless to say, I put all my clothes in the dryer first. It is a humiliation I will never forget, and one I hope you can avoid.

As someone living alone, I do laundry probably twice a week. One of those days is on the weekend since I am home for enough time to keep it going in the background all day long. I simply do not generate that much wash—whatever I wore to work (which often goes to the dry cleaner because it is tailored, silk, or the tag says "dry clean only"), clothes I wore to exercise in, pajamas, underwear, towels from baths and showers, and maybe a t-shirt and yoga pants.

To make life easier, here are the steps and a strategy to doing laundry effectively. It's a life skill that I aspire to be better at doing regularly, but this should help:

- *Sort all of your dirty clothes and linen into loads.* When deciding which laundry to do first, sort everything into piles to determine how many loads you will need to do. Here are some categories to sort your laundry by:

  - light colors (whites and grays)

  - dark colors (super-bright things, red things)

  - things that require a mesh bag for washing (bras and other delicates)

  - linen (blankets and sheets)

  - towels.

This means several loads of laundry, so 1 assume that's about six hours of washing and drying while 1 am doing other stuff throughout the day. 1 like to put all the light-colored things in one pile and dark (and red) colored things in another so there are no dye transfers (nothing worse than turning white shirts into pink ones). For special washes (i.e., lacey, delicate things, or garments 1 love so much 1 don't want them getting messed up with anything else), 1 do things 1 don't want to wrinkle on their own, so 1 can hang them up to dry immediately, and don't throw them into the dryer by mistake. 1 also do a separate load for my sheets each week as well as a separate wash for the pink blanket on my bed. Finally, 1 do a separate load for towels.

Depending on your chosen washing machine and dryer settings, a load can take a few minutes or up to an hour. If 1 do it all on the same day, it's just hours (my washer/dryer is ancient, and the dryer takes at an hour), so 1 try to time it that 1 do my sheets and pillowcases on the same day as my blanket. 1 might do my towels after a shower. Or I'll do the things that need to be hung before 1 go to bed, so they can dry overnight.

- *Try to remove stains before putting anything in the wash.*
  If you notice anything has a stain on it, now is a good
  time to use a stain remover pen or solution. Let it sit
  and follow the instructions before putting it in the wash.

- *Load in the detergent and any other products.* To get started
  on doing laundry, you need detergent. You can also use
  some fabric softeners, so your clothes feel more sensory-
  friendly and smell good afterwards. Since measuring
  detergent is kind of a mystery, I personally recommend
  buying laundry detergent pods since you don't have to
  pour anything or worry about having a load of wash
  with way too many suds in it. Set an alarm (or pray your
  washing machine makes a noise when a load is complete)
  for when your laundry is done in the wash. Then, you
  can immediately move it to the dryer.

- *Move the wet laundry to the dryer or hang it up.* Don't forget to move things out of the washing machine to dry!
  If you leave things in the washer for too long, they get
  moldy or smell funny from sitting in a dark, wet place.

  You'll need to put some items in the dryer. Use
  whatever setting is most efficient or is instructed on the
  garments (e.g., tumble dry low). Be sure to set an alarm or
  wait for the dryer to beep when your stuff is done drying,
  so you can take it out and then fold it.

  Other stuff, like nice shirts, bras, and other garments,
  should be hung up to dry.

  When your laundry is done drying, it is always a nice
  feeling to have warm, clean clothes. I love the feeling of
  a warm blanket fresh out of the dryer!

- *Iron anything that needs to be ironed.* I am not adept whatsoever at using an iron and ironing board (my ironing
  board is collecting dust, probably), so I save this for very
  special garments and things that look super-wrinkly,

or bring those things home so my mom helps me. No shame. My knowledge ends at knowing to use low heat settings to avoid burning myself or wrecking the fabric.

- *Fold your clean clothes and linens.* Fold your clothes when they are dry and put everything back in your closet or in the drawers where your stuff belongs. That way, your clean stuff doesn't get wrinkled.

- *What to do if you have to use your complex's machines or go to a laundromat.* If you don't have a washing machine or dryer in your house or apartment and have shared washing machines in your apartment complex or have to use a laundromat, be sure to move everything as soon as humanly possible so other people don't move your stuff to use the machines or even steal your stuff!

KEY TAKEAWAY

- Don't let your laundry pile up in that sad corner in your room forever. It'll become so overwhelming that you will never end up doing it, and when you do finally commit to sorting and organizing it, your executive functioning (and patience) will be so thoroughly tested, you'll never want to do it again. Just trust me on this one.

Safety

Part of living on your own is also being safe. Physical safety in your home seems kind of simple, but plenty of things take work and mindfulness, especially when it comes to visitors and preparing for the event of an emergency like a natural disaster or house fire (kitchens can be dangerous)—or doing your part to prevent a crime.

Unexplainable emergencies, natural disasters, and power outages

Here's the thing about emergencies: they are routine disruptions we do not get nearly enough time to adapt to and account for—we didn't get the opportunity to truly prepare for shortages of toilet paper during the coronavirus pandemic, for instance. I grew up in Florida, so having emergency plans for hurricane season no matter where I lived was just a fact of life and something to plan for each summer and autumn. Outside of the panic of the news, I learned at an early age to regularly have the "essentials" stocked at any time.

No matter what types of emergencies might crop up, there are some essentials you should have in your home, including favorite foods and snacks, bottled water, toilet paper, alcohol wipes or other sanitizers, and oil/gas for generators or your car in case you need to evacuate or go somewhere else. When widespread emergencies happen, people panic, stores and gas stations become overwhelming, and crucial supplies are suddenly nowhere in sight. Avoid the stress and potential meltdowns: have this stuff in your home, no matter what.

During major storms or a bad stroke of luck, you might lose power or electricity. Don't panic since chances are it is affecting you and your entire neighborhood or apartment building. You can either call the power company to report the outage, or you will be updated on the status of the outage. To keep safe during and after a power outage:

- *Keep your fridge and freezer closed.* Even if you're hungry, you probably won't be able to heat anything without power, so try to limit how often you open the fridge or freezer doors. This will maintain the cold so you do not have to throw out any frozen or refrigerated food. If the outage lasts for more than 4 hours, you should throw away perishable, refrigerated foods like meat, poultry, fish, or eggs. Frozen food, depending on the product and how much food is in your freezer, can last 24–48 hours, so you most likely won't have to worry too much there.

- *Keep your cell phone charged.* Since power outages also result in loss of internet and landline phone services, your cell phone is likely your only form of contact with the outside world. But Haley, you might say, we don't have power! Charge your phone through your laptop or a portable battery pack or charger. Try to avoid using your phone for nonessential communication, excessive web browsing, social media, or gaming, so you can preserve battery power if need be.

- *Do not use a generator inside of the house or a closed indoor space like a garage.* I am aware that most people probably do not own a generator, but on the off-chance you do, this powerful, temporary restoration of power can be either a lifesaver or a life-ender. Having weathered more than a few severe tropical storms and hurricanes in my life, my family has more than one useable generator. In Florida, somebody usually runs one inside after losing power in a hurricane, and it ends in either hospitalization or death because of the gases the generator emits. Generators must be used and plugged in outdoors because carbon monoxide can quickly be trapped in an indoor or enclosed space. If you own a generator and need power (my family will do this to save perishables within our fridge and freezer, and then maybe use the microwave to heat food, or be able to charge important electronics like cell phones for safety purposes), you can run yours outside with the exhaust facing away from the indoors.

If you do not have a generator, you can plug electronics into your car or other portable power supply.

Preventative measures

Some safety is not just in case of an emergency, but also for preventing crimes or dangerous situations from occurring at home.

If you are able to do so, invest in a home security system (especially if you live alone or in a big city). Do-it-yourself systems can be purchased online and you can set up security sensors for the front door and other points of entry, water heaters to prevent leaks, or cameras, and you can register them with your local police or fire department, so they are automatically contacted in the event of a supposed break-in or other catastrophic event. You can go as secure as you'd like including cameras, but a motion sensor can also catch suspicious activity when you aren't home, and your alarm system is armed when you're away.

This sounds like common sense to a lot of people, but remember to lock your front door. Lock the door if you are leaving the house. Lock it when you're inside so no unexpected visitors show up and are able to enter. Keep a spare key somewhere that you know where it is but that might not be a first impulse to look for a stranger (they always look under the doormat).

Expected and unexpected visitors

If you live in a gated community or somewhere with a concierge or security at a desk, door, or gatehouse, they will call you on the phone whenever a visitor arrives, wanting to see you. Such visitors are likely delivery workers for food/errands you ordered or friends you invited over. If you live in a place without security, be sure to check through the front door peephole before opening the door or letting a stranger in. If you are high-tech, camera security doorbell systems like Ring might be an alternative too (aside from the privacy concerns some folks may have). If someone you aren't expecting is at the door, talk through the door, keep it locked, and if necessary, call a neighbor, security, or the police for help to safeguard yourself and your neighbors.

THE SENSORY OVERWHELMING GROCERY STORE AND OTHER ERRANDS

One of the things that probably changed most from when I was in college going to the dining hall and occasionally to restaurants to now, when I am fully on my own and working, was how much I go to the grocery store as my main errand. I always find myself in need of something from the deli counter, a bottle of wine in case I have guests, laundry detergent, snacks, or a craving for a tub of ice cream and wanting to have fresh bananas in the house for breakfast the next morning.

You might also need to do things like go to a home improvement store for major repairs or things like getting light bulbs, tools, or other maintenance items. You might buy cookware from a more general store or a specialty boutique. Or, you can always do what I do to simplify the process, and order online. But the one errand I cannot avoid no matter what (and mostly because I don't want someone else to pick out food for me): the grocery store, or the one thing that an Amazon Prime membership does not fully cover (though it does give me discounts at Whole Foods Market, which are appreciated).

The other great thing about supermarkets and grocery stores, to me at least, is you can *knock out a bunch of errands at once by going to them*. My dad is a pharmacist and pointed out that *most supermarkets have pharmacies inside of them*. This means you can likely call in a prescription before going and pick it up while you're shopping for groceries, which can save you a lot of time. Using grocery store pharmacies is also advantageous since they are smaller and not very crowded. Similarly, *the customer service counter sells stamps*. They won't mail things out for you like the post office, but you do not have to order online or go to a post office to buy stamps (I know, who'd guess stamps are hiding in the back with the cigarettes and lottery tickets?). Depending on your grocery store, you might also be able to get money orders or other random needs met.

There is one thing about grocery stores though—I, like many other autistics, do not like going to them. Dr Elizabeth Shea, the clinical psychologist who specializes in food-related issues and also works with people on the autism spectrum, also understands why grocery stores are hard for us. There are often screaming and crying children. The shopping carts clatter down linoleum floors. The aisles always seem to be jam-packed with people. There are so many different foods and products to choose from! Dr Shea acknowledges that not every autistic young person has been shopping on their own before. Parents or caregivers might be the ones who are buying and preparing food for us. Grocery stores also circle back to some of our food-related issues discussed earlier. Dr Shea has explained to me that learning to go grocery shopping with a friend, roommate, or family member can help us get used to the sensory experience and tasks we're supposed to do.

Grocery stores and supermarkets can be overwhelming, but we're always hungry and in need of food and essentials no matter where we live, so here are some strategies (thanks to my many trips, at least once a week, to the grocery store) that I've wrangled up with some help from my mom, who arguably ends up at the supermarket more than I do:

- *Make a list of what you need.* My mom always has a list on the counter that she adds to throughout the week or few days in between visits to the grocery store where she adds what she needs based on what we used as a family, what expired, or what she wants to cook or bake. I just list out the things I am craving or would like to eat, or stuff I'd like to have in the house in case of emergency. I also like to have snacks just in case, and sometimes need the reminder from a list to replenish my supply. A grocery list helps you stay on task, move throughout the store strategically, and avoid getting stuff you don't actually want or need simply because it's there and looks tempting.

Some of us get stuck on a particular brand or packaging of items we need, and that can be stressful! Some autistics have that desire for sameness, but, as Dr Shea explains, supermarkets give us examples of products that "though [they] might appear different, are actually quite similar." This is a great way to discover new brands, shapes, or foods that feel safe and similar, while also giving us what we want when it is not always an option.

Sometimes, the thing you want or need might not be there. In that case, you might make a decision whether to skip it completely or substitute it with something else. I am a Diet Coke® drinker. It is a fact most people know about me, but if the store is out of Diet Coke® and all that is there is Diet Pepsi® (which is not my first choice), I might momentarily feel a little nervous or unsure of what to do. However, I would know since the Diet Pepsi® is located right next to where the Diet Coke® would be, that they are likely very similar and that would signal it is okay.

- *Have a store navigation strategy.* I didn't know this until my mom mentioned it, but nearly every grocery store or supermarket has a similar layout. The outside aisles of the store are the ones with perishables: the produce sections, the bakery and breads, the deli counter, the meat and poultry section. The inside aisles are all dry goods. Keeping this in mind can help if you just have to make a quick dash in to get one or two things. You can also use this to have a mental map and plan to execute in order to avoid the crowds and overwhelm.

Part of your store navigation strategy might also be going at "off peak" times to minimize crowds and noise. You can take your time and make this errand far less stressful. When I was in school, I'd go mid-afternoon—after the lunch rush, but before people would get off from work. The most crowded times are mid-morning (before work or when parents drop their kids off at school), lunchtime, and after work/rush hour. For working folks, the least crowded times to go are when the store first opens or before it closes (though if you go late at night before closing, be extra conscious and safe about your surroundings).

Dr Shea also knows that going to supermarkets and grocery stores can be stressful, and recommends having an exit strategy as part of your store navigation strategy.

- *Check expiration dates on products.* Most people do this after the fact, unfortunately, or when things have been sitting in their homes for too long. Grocery stores have a tendency to put items that are more likely to expire soon right up front, hoping to capitalize on the convenience. Check the dates on the products and look for the ones that'll last the longest, unless it's something perishable like produce that you'll end up eating or using immediately.

- *Look online or in the newspapers/circulation ads for coupons.* Other sections in this book talk a lot about saving and spending money, but one way to stick to your budget (and possibly get more product) is to look for coupons from either the supermarket itself or the product manufacturers. This might be when it is helpful to buy a little bit in bulk as well. Groceries and food are one of the biggest expenses we have, and being able to cut down in some way is always helpful.

- *If you absolutely do not want to (or cannot) go to a store, there are apps and delivery services that will bring groceries and supplies for you.* You will still have to pick the products you need, but if you made a list, this will be infinitely easier. Keep in mind that these apps and services, like Instacart and Shipt (or Ocado in the UK, for example) cost more money than going yourself because of inflated prices, delivery fees, and tips. However, it can make your life a little easier if you are low on spoons (see BBC News 2013), time, executive functioning skills, or feel overwhelmed in stores or by the idea of going. And this is also where my other errands come in handy too since those are items I'll be more likely to order online. I can't say I ever picked out light bulbs in person, which brings me to my next point.

HOW MANY AUTISTICS DOES IT TAKE TO CHANGE A LIGHT BULB?

I am not a tall person. I am about 5'3" and I have nice, high ceilings. I also have dainty chandeliers and lighting fixtures with tiny and big bulbs alike hanging over my bed in my bedroom and over my couch. When the light bulbs above my bathroom mirror burn out (which they do regularly), I am suddenly part of a human jungle gym, standing on countertops and chairs in an effort to put in fresh light bulbs. When it comes to my living room and bedroom, no number of chairs can save me. What is a girl like me to do—live with a lack of light in my house?

This is usually about the time I call my dad, who will bring his ladder. If I had a house and not a one-bedroom apartment,

I would probably have a ladder in my garage or something. If I had a roommate, they might be able to help me because they are more mechanically savvy or perhaps taller than I am.

Sure, moral of the story: have a step ladder or something to boost your height. Also, when it comes to home maintenance, make sure to have an essentials toolbox or toolkit on board. Have some nails, Command™ strips (to hang stuff up), extra light bulbs, screwdrivers, wrenches—the basics for repairs that don't require calling someone more skilled to help with. Have a few quick-catch supplies like solution to pour down a clogged drain or a plunger for a clog in the toilet. These things can end up saving you a lot of stress and anguish over getting a repair person or contacting your landlord.

Important people to have phone numbers for

I am not a savvy person when it comes to home repairs or maintenance that is beyond me or my dad, who is, in my opinion, a Mr Fix-It who lives less than an hour away. But some things are beyond both of our control, and in the five years I have lived in the same place, I've had a rotating cast of characters on speed dial for varying issues. There are a few people I think everyone should have access to if there is a job or home repair too big for you to handle; sure, there are more specialized folks, and you might need them too, but here are the basics:

- *Building management company or superintendent.* Building management can answer all sorts of random questions you have, and they also inform you of construction, planned outages, and other major issues.

- *Air conditioning or heater repair company.* My air conditioning unit and heater have both had issues no matter where I have lived in my life, and being able to quickly get someone to assess the situation and make repairs has been a blessing, so I don't sweat to death between a warm house and the sweltering Florida heat and humidity.

- *Handyman.* I have thankfully only had to call a handyman for help with a project once, but this person can help with minor to major household projects, painting, floor repair—you name it. If you live in an apartment building, your building might have someone helpful on staff or you can easily get a recommendation. I got recommended mine from a former tenant.

- *Plumber.* Chances are, you will get at least one mystery clog or toilet issue in your adult life, and it'll be beyond your plunger's reach.

- *At least one of your neighbors.* It wasn't until a leak was coming from upstairs that I had the number of the person who lived above me, but now that I do, I know to call them if my bathroom ceiling is leaking. I also have the numbers of some of my other nearby neighbors in case of an emergency or a building-wide issue. It's also good to have their numbers in case you need a favor, like asking them to hold a package for you while you are away or something.

- *Housekeeper.* If you need help tidying up, having a reputable, trustworthy person can be immensely helpful. You can find a good housekeeper through a friend, word of mouth, or services like TaskRabbit, Handy, or Care.com. You'll need to schedule this person in advance—not a quick emergency phone call like others on this list.

- *Power company.* While in an emergency you might lose power or electricity, you will want to have access to the power company to report the outage or get them to send people to investigate the source of the outage. As an aside, *you might also want an electrician* in case of any other electrical issues that aren't just a major widespread loss of power.

Being a parent to a plant, dog, or cat

I have always grown up around animals. A dog greeted me at my house the day I came home from the hospital as a newborn. A cat entered my life a few years ago. However, I am not very good at taking care of myself, let alone another living creature, so my pets live with my parents, and not me.

Animals like dogs have always been helpful socially. Whenever we'd walk our family dog, people would stop to talk or pet the dog. I've made friends bonding over standard poodles as a kid, and even just had conversations with nice people who wanted to talk about my dog and stop to give him a pet or two. It might not be a perfect or the main reason to be a pet owner, but pets do help with social lives (on top of giving you an excuse to leave a situation: "I'm sorry, I have to walk my dog!").

To autistic people, animals might be more than just pets or family members. They may be critical parts of our care and access teams. *Emotional support animals* are pets that we might have to help us ease anxiety, and can run the gamut from dogs to exotic animals. Under the law, emotional support animals are allowed in homes, apartments, and in airports and on airplanes. They are able to provide comfort to multiple people. More extreme perhaps than an emotional support animal is a *service dog or service animal*, which is specifically trained to help in situations like meltdowns. Under federal law, service animals are allowed to accompany you everywhere. While I have never had a service animal, it is important to understand that when you see them (and they are working), they are not pets and you should not distract them from assisting their humans with disabilities.

Some people see pets as precursors to having children, wanting to see how they fare taking care of something other than themselves or a partner, perhaps. While I'm not at this phase of life, I've seen it numerous times.

Whether you have a pet, emotional support animal, or a service animal, pets and animals require care. You have to remember to regularly feed them, clean after them, walk them, and spend time with them. Animals are a commitment—especially more traditional pets like dogs and cats—because they live a long time. Animals also require money for food, vet visits, and in some cases, grooming, or even boarding if you go on vacation and don't have friends or family to watch your pet while you're away. You might also not be able to live in some places that have strict pet policies restricting weight or certain types of animals, like my apartment building, which does not allow dogs (unless they are emotional support or service animals), or others that charge additional fees for dogs and cats. Basically, a lot goes into the decision to have animals in your home.

I am not ready to take on the responsibility of having my own dog or cat live with me, but that's okay! I love hanging out with other people's animals and the ones I grew up with. When I am thinking about being ready, however, I do think that I might get a living plant to water and make sure it has sunlight exposure as compared with the fake ones I currently decorate my house with.

HAVING ROOMMATES

Let me tell you the story of my first and only roommate. Like many 18-year-olds living in college dorms, I wanted a "typical college experience," so I wanted to have a roommate. My mom contacted the campus disability center and they let me interview older female students as a potential roommate; I wanted someone who was on campus for at least a year since I felt I could learn from a "big sister"-type person. While I liked my roommate, and we were friends after the housing department first introduced us, things quickly took a turn for the worse. My roommate and I regularly had disagreements about everything—our sleep and study habits, if we brought friends over to our dorm, and even what food we kept in our fridge.

I moved out within six months and have then either lived at home with my parents or completely on my own ever since that brief stint when I was 18 years old. I enjoy my own space and privacy, but sometimes I like visitors from out of town and overnight guests. Having a roommate is a decision you might want to make. Having roommates can help you save money on rent and live in a bigger apartment—or help you meet new people if you are moving to a new city.

Not a lot of people outside of dorm life and school situations are assigned purely random roommates, where they are matched and are somehow given each other's contact information and live in the same shared room. As an adult, your housemates might be your parents or family members. If you are living away from family, there are several ways you can get a roommate:

- *You and a friend you already have might choose to live together.* A lot of people I know often choose to live with their already-existing friends because they know each other well and have similar personalities and habits. However, be mindful that living with someone might be different than just being friends with them and seeing them on occasion.

- *You might choose to move in with a romantic partner.* Depending on where your relationship is, you and your partner might choose to move in and live together to advance your relationship to the next stage or to save money. While I have never permanently lived with someone I have dated, I feel like it might be a good idea to have a plan in case you break up. It might be weird being stuck in a year-long lease with someone who becomes your ex.

- *You might move in with someone else you don't know who is also looking for a roommate.* You might be introduced to potential roommates through mutual friends, the internet, or a message board of sorts. Be sure this is something you feel comfortable with and spend some time together before deciding to sign a lease and live under the same roof. When I was in law school, a lot of law students relocating to the area—before they met—would agree to be roommates because they knew they were all moving, looking for housing, and would be classmates anyway.

- *You might live with a family member also looking to move.* In my apartment building, there were two brothers who lived together because they were attending the same university but graduated a year apart. You never know—it can be a good idea to live with a family member you already know if you are both living in the same city or your plans align, like those brothers' plans did.

Getting along and sharing responsibilities

When you live with someone else, like any other relationship, you will probably have disagreements and need to set some ground rules and learn to communicate better with each other about things related to your shared space. When I look back on my roommate experiences, most of what went down other than incompatible personalities was just that we did not talk about how we lived and what we expected of one another.

- *Set rules and routines together.* You might have similar living habits, or you might not. Are you allowed to share dishes and eat each other's food? How will you split the rent—in half, or will the person with the bigger bedroom end up paying more—and which of you is giving the money to the landlord each month? Who will take out the trash and who is responsible for certain utilities? How clean do you each expect the house to be? Do you feel super-opinionated when your roommate's romantic partner stays over multiple days a week since they don't live with you two or pay up? These are some of the many things to consider talking to your roommate about before and during the time you're living together.

You will want to set some ground rules about each other's stuff, hosting guests, how and when to contact each other when you're not at home (sometimes a quick text to say you'll be home late might be helpful to avoid them worrying about you, while in other situations a phone call might be more appropriate). Decide how you will manage and split maintenance, grocery shopping, utilities and rent, and household chores to avoid disagreements. Make sure to do your part! Keep in mind these boundaries might look different if you are living with a romantic partner.

You might also want to set rules about what you are willing to share. Your roommate might have really cute or comfortable clothes you want to borrow. Of course, ask for permission, but maybe you might have a rule that it is okay to borrow certain things from each other as long as you put them back where they came from (but no stealing each other's stuff!).

To help solidify the rules and routines you set together, maybe write them up, so you can reference them. Or, if you want something less formal, think of how you plan to communicate about living space arrangement stuff. As you settle into a rhythm, the rules can change— just communicate openly and honestly with each other.

- *Communicate with each other.* Based on the rules and routines you set, open communication can make a world of difference. Rather than fighting and threatening to move out, you and your roommate can figure out the best ways to solve conflict, hold each other accountable, and follow your rules and routines.

Make sure all communication is respectful. You do not want to hurt each other's feelings. Something you should figure out is how you best communicate—maybe having a weekly check-in on how things are going around the house might solve issues before they become big and someone bottles them up. You may have to compromise on some things to keep the peace with each other.

Financially Supporting Yourself

EAGER FOR EMPLOYMENT

You did it! You graduated school, and are ready to spread your wings and fly out into the world of having a job. Sadly, the deck is stacked against autistic people looking to enter the workforce. Only 58 percent of young autistic people have work experience after high school and into their early twenties, and adults with intellectual and developmental disabilities (including autism) have an 85 percent unemployment rate, according to a 2018 Autism Society of America briefing (Optum, Inc. 2018).

Young autistic adults out of high school or college might receive transitional employment services through a state's vocational rehabilitation (VR) program. This is a federally funded program that is administered by the state for adults with disabilities to obtain jobs and stay employed. Each state has a VR agency that provides employment service support and assessments that can lead to developing an Individual Plan for Employment (IPE). Through a VR program, autistic adults who qualify may get assessed on skills, help from job coaches and counselors with interviewing and job skills, job placement and assistance services, counsel, training, or even financial assistance to have assistive technologies like augmented and alternative communication devices.

Other programs that help employ autistic people are vast. There are government programs like the federal Workforce Recruitment Program (WRP) for recent graduates and college students with disabilities looking to enter the federal government. The WRP is a valuable resource to connect you to public and private sector employers. If you are a student or recent graduate, connect with your university career office about the WRP.

The private sector has autism hiring initiatives across major corporations like Microsoft, EY, JPMorgan, and others. Some places almost exclusively hire autistic people, like Ultranauts and Auticon. Other places in your community may be social enterprises, run by local entrepreneurs to employ autistic and similarly neurodivergent people within the community. Other nonprofits and organizations may run what are known as sheltered workshops, which only employ people with disabilities and, if they have authorization from the government, can pay employees less than the minimum wage (this is a whole policy and disability rights issue in and of itself; if you are interested in finding out more, see Luterman 2020).

No matter how you want to go about getting a job—working alongside other autistic people, in competitive, integrated settings, starting a business, or working for a small business—the possibilities are infinite. For the parents, supporters, employers, and allies reading this: we want to work! Working for pay is one of the most empowering things on the road to feeling independent and achieving the financial stability many of us view as a barrier to independent living.

The evolving job search and feeling qualified

Depending on your skill set, education, and dreams, job possibilities are endless. Autistic people of all skill sets and abilities work in every single industry across all sorts of employment settings. Some are entrepreneurs and self-employed. Others work in social enterprises.

Luckily for you, neurodiversity in the workplace is a growing trend in competitive, integrated employment settings where there are workers with and without disabilities. Companies have continued to recognize that neurodiverse workers are innovators; in some cases, such as at German technology giant SAP, a neurodiverse team saved them nearly $40 million with a technological fix (Austin and Pisano 2017). With major companies across industries purposely looking to recruit autistic workers through programs such as Specialisterne USA and the Stanford Neurodiversity Project, the possibilities for autistic job seekers are endless.

So is disability inclusion. According to data from Accenture (Lindzon 2019), companies that are disability inclusion champions and hire disabled and neurodivergent people average higher shareholder returns (translation: their investors make more money) and the companies have higher revenues.

As a young autistic person, job hunting can be intimidating. It often feels like every job posting wants someone with years and years of experience, a fancy degree, excellent people skills, and other unattainable qualifications. Here is the thing: a lot of those requirements (if they are not essential to doing the job well) are a wish list that employers have. You are more qualified than you think you are.

Surviving the recruiting and hiring process

As an autistic person, going through the job application process can be an absolute minefield. There are all sorts of formalities, like resumes, cover letters, interviews, offers, and negotiations for salary and benefits involved. There is the forever question of disclosing autism and the best time and strategy to request accommodations. According to a study from Steven Kapp and his colleagues, neurotypical people regularly misunderstand and misinterpret autistic people's behaviors (Kapp *et al.* 2019). We communicate more directly and use different body language.

Building your resume

A resume is a one- or two-page document that summarizes and describes your educational background, experience, and skills. Recruiters and employers review resumes in order to determine if you might be a good fit for the job. Sometimes, artificial intelligence (AI) or computers will review your resume to decide if you can advance to an interview with humans.

Deciding what to put on your resume might be a difficult task, especially if you are very involved in your community or have a lot of education or work experience. Something I liked to do early on was create a LinkedIn profile—this is usually a good way for employers and recruiters to get a snapshot of you online, and you can put far more information on that than you can on a resume. LinkedIn is almost like a very long resume in that you put your education, experience, skills, projects, and accomplishments on it. I like to use it as a "running list" of sorts, and then I pick and choose the highlights from LinkedIn for a shorter, more concise document, since I can't list every article I've ever written or some of my experience is less relevant for either autism-related work or legal work.

To get started, you can download a bunch of helpful resume

templates online for the formatting. No matter what template you're using, though, you'll have the following sections on your resume:

- *Contact information.* This should be at the top of your resume and include your name, an email address you check regularly (be sure it is a professional-sounding email address; if not, set one up through Gmail with your name and possibly a number or two after it. If you have your own website, you can always do a branded email address, like john@johndoe.com), a physical mailing address (some recommend just your city, state, and zip code, but I think a physical mailing address is okay too), and a phone number (your cell phone number, most likely).

- *Education.* You should list your degree and what college or university you attended, and when you graduated. For me this, might look like "Bachelor of Science, Psychology | University of Florida, Gainesville, FL" and at the end of the line, "2015." If you are still a student, you can write "Expected" before your anticipated year and month of graduation. If you went to college or university, do not list where you went to high school. You can also list any clubs or organizations you were a part of when you were in school (especially if they are relevant or you were part of the leadership), or awards and honors you received. Or, if you have them, you can also list licenses and certifications related to the skill set and job you're applying for.

- *Work and volunteer experience.* This is the crux of your resume. List your experiences from most recent to oldest. Include the position title, name of the company or organization, location (city and state), month and year when you started followed by the month and year you left (if you are still there, write "present"), and a few bullet points of what your responsibilities were in each role. Try to limit the work and volunteer experience to what is most important—the older you get, the more you'll trim off the smaller volunteer roles or jobs you didn't stay in for very long. That way, your resume isn't longer than a page or two. You'll still want to keep those descriptions of past jobs and experiences handy in case you need them for a different resume.

Depending on the industry or if you're looking for entry-level jobs, you might also have these sections, too. Or you might also have a linked portfolio of your work for fine arts, journalism, or other creative-adjacent industries if a job requires you have work to show.

- *Publications.* This might be a portfolio thing, but if you are entering a research field or have any scholarly publications, books, or notable writing related to your industry worth showcasing, you might put it here. I have always had a publication section on my resume because I was a writer and most of my experience is writing-related. I also include my books and law review publications on legal industry resumes to distinguish myself as an expert.

- *Summary.* I have never written a summary on a resume before, but, according to the resume guide from the Organization for Autism Research (OAR) for self-advocates (n.d.), this should be directly below your contact information. OAR writes that a summary statement is "a short paragraph placed at the top of a resume that highlights your professional skills and experience." It is a quick snapshot of who you are, and if you lack skills, the ones you hope to learn from the job you're applying for.

- *Skills.* I don't write a skills section on my resume because I have a lot of experience at this point, but it was something I did while in college and applying for internships.

Also, I was not in an industry with super-specialized knowledge, like coding languages, or I was not fluent in multiple languages. You can also do keyword personality traits, like saying you are attentive to detail or organized.

- *Writing sample.* This might be a portfolio thing, but in some industries, you might also need to have a writing sample. For the legal industry, lawyers and law clerks are almost always asked for this—it's usually a legal document or pleading on which we were the primary author. If you're applying for a marketing job or other career field that requests this, see what exactly they are looking for, since writing for the internet, writing for journalism, writing for court, and writing for school are all very different things that have different skill sets.

- *References.* Some resumes and recruiters want you to list a few professional or personal references. Give those people's names and information if they agree to it and if it belongs here; otherwise, it might not be necessary, or you might provide references on another part of the job application.

If you think there is a chance the recruiter is using AI or robots to screen through resumes, use keywords in describing your past roles. To figure out what is important for that particular job, look at the responsibilities or essential duties or functions of the job. These are the things that are most crucial to being successful in the role.

Even if you are not actively seeking a job, keep your resume updated. It will ultimately save you time, and you will easily remember important things as they happen to you. This is where LinkedIn also comes in—updating resumes and LinkedIn will make your life easier if the time comes to apply for jobs in the future, or to keep connected with professional contacts and allow for the updates to notify them rather than have to initiate new conversations yourself about your achievements, job changes, etc.

Writing a cover letter

A cover letter is the other half of the set along with a resume when applying for jobs; you'll send it by email or upload it onto the application to the person requesting it. Cover letters help you stand out as they are often the first document in your application materials that a recruiter might read and will make them excited to interview you. Unlike a resume, you should tailor your cover letter to each place you apply to because there might be certain skills you want to highlight, and you should personalize who it is addressed to depending on the person, business, or organization you are applying to. In the header, you should put your contact information to match your resume (after all, the two documents are complementing each other), and date, and address the letter to the contact person at the company, beginning with a salutation. You'll want to express interest in the position, highlighting your skills and qualifications (and the ones you would like to grow within the position). Your job here is to say how your qualifications make you a great fit for the job.

If you feel it is appropriate, you might disclose you're autistic in a cover letter. I do not personally think this is the place to do so, however, unless it is absolutely relevant to the job, but there is more within this section on disclosure, the pros and cons, and when to do so.

Interviewing

You did it! You wrote an excellent resume and cover letter, and now a human (hopefully, as compared with an AI screener) wants to interview you! Job interviews are intimidating because it is never completely clear what an interviewer might be looking for or judging you on. While interviewers are assessing if you're a good fit based on technical qualifications and experiences, they are also looking to see if you belong socially as a culture fit and have the interpersonal skills needed to succeed. Some interviewers want the best technical fit for the job and others want someone who is both professional and someone they can see themselves being friends with. Every place is different.

During job interviews, there are many ways we communicate differently than our neurotypical counterparts, and are expected to act like them. Many autistic people feel deeply uncomfortable with eye contact, feeling that they are being stared at or are staring at someone in a way that detracts focus from the conversation. Yet in job interviews, recruiters and hiring decision-makers view eye contact as a way to determine if someone is being honest. It becomes uncomfortable having to choose between forced eye contact and possibly missing something important. Other forms of fidgeting or stimming, like hand flapping or clicking a pen, can be seen as unprofessional or like we are uninterested, but for autistics, and depending on the individual, these actions might reduce anxiety, convey enthusiasm, or allow for a focus on verbal communication. Recognizing disclosure of autism may be appropriate in order to have the other person feel more empathetic or so you can receive reasonable accommodations during the process or later, on the job.

If you have an autism diagnosis, you are able to receive job accommodations during the interview process. You might need to provide health or medical documentation as requested to receive a reasonable accommodation. The Job Accommodation Network (JAN), a project funded by the US Department of Labor, offers these ideas as sample accommodations. I think they can be helpful depending on what your needs are, and here's why:

- *Requesting fewer interviewers.* Panel interviews can be intimidating, and having fewer interviewers can help with differences in social skills (Whetzel 2010).

- *Requesting that the first interview be conducted by phone.* Some of us have severe phone anxiety, so this is probably not a great accommodation for everyone. In today's world, you might also be able to request an interview over text, instant messaging, or video conference. An interview that isn't face-to-face can also ease some of the subjective criteria interviewers look for, such as eye contact, and allow them (and you) to focus more on your answers to their questions and have the opportunity to show what you know.

- *Requesting a copy of the interview questions to be provided in advance.* JAN suggests questions be provided in advance. That way, autistic job seekers might not feel anxious the first time they hear something that can limit on-the-spot thinking in a way that doesn't reflect the applicant's knowledge or experience. Seeing the questions in advance can also help you better prepare questions to ask the interviewer and not expect any surprises.

- *Requesting that the interview occur at a specific time of day.* If the disability involves limitations in concentration, focus, or energy and fatigue, the time of day individuals are at their best may vary (Whetzel 2010).

Disclosing autism

When I was applying for jobs before graduating law school, one question on applications always filled me with anxiety: "Are you a person with a disability?" The answers to check off were especially unhelpful—"Yes," which might have opened me up to bias and discrimination, "No," which is a flat-out lie (and being dishonest on an application is bad, right?), and "Prefer not to disclose," which to me was a polite way of saying "Yes, but I don't want to tell you right now." What was I to do? I ultimately went with "Yes" because I am openly autistic by virtue of all of the other work I do. I don't see myself as neurotypical, so "No" doesn't feel right, on top of the fact that a quick search of my name online nets you a ton of results about the autism-related work I've done, all including the fact that I am autistic. I am sure that being open might make some employers do a double-take, but others, like my first employer once I graduated, saw my autism as a strength and something to celebrate in the workplace.

Autism disclosure is always an individual decision, situation to situation, person to person. You may choose to disclose you are autistic in a cover letter, interview, when you have a job offer in hand, after starting, if or when you need a reasonable accommodation at work—or never. That decision is entirely up to you.

- *Consider who you want to know that you're autistic.* You might not care if your colleagues know you're autistic, or you might only want your direct supervisor to know. Historically, while all of my colleagues and supervisors would know I am autistic, the amount of information I would share would vary. I would usually give more details to my supervisor in case I needed an accommodation. I avoided sharing too much with colleagues because I wanted to be treated and perceived as an equal; one of the fears plenty of disabled folks have about disclosure is being seen as receiving special treatment or being a target of workplace harassment or bullying.

- *Disclosing is necessary to receive accommodations in the workplace.* When I spoke to Emily Shuman, Deputy Director of the Rocky Mountain ADA Center, for an article on disclosure for *Fast Company*, she told me that the "best thing to do is disclose that you have a disability when you realize that you cannot perform the essential functions of your job because of your disability and need an accommodation" (quoted in Moss 2020). While some of this might sound like legal jargon to you, it means you need an accommodation to do the stuff your job description says you have to be able to do.

JAN (n.d.) has suggestions for sample accommodations at work that might be helpful for autistic workers like you. You can request to use noise-cancelling headphones to help with sensory situations, breaks, fidget devices, flexible scheduling, and more.

- *If you have a spotty or unique employment history, disclosure might help you.* In a law review article detailing the legal issues of autism spectrum disorders in the workplace, Wendy F. Hensel, a law professor at Georgia State University, concluded that disclosure earlier in the job process can help explain unique resumes autistics have that show "an inordinate number of jobs, gaps between jobs, or a long history of self-employment" (Hensel 2017)—basically, an autism diagnosis helps employers make sense of what typically can be concerning behavior before an interview. Autism colors in the lines, so to speak, and helps humanize us throughout the hiring process.

Some experts and autistics agree that honesty might be the best policy. Disclosure can potentially create a more favorable perception for you as a job candidate because it explains an inconsistent job history and allows employers the time and knowledge to best prepare and accommodate someone on the spectrum. Disclosure also makes differences in employment history or interpersonal skills seem secondary to an autistic job candidate's abilities and potential to succeed within a position (Hensel 2017).

I tend to agree with Professor Hensel's research and conclusions that honesty is the best policy, at least for me. I always feel like I'm lying or hiding something if I don't disclose, and it might even lead to more favorable outcomes in certain places. It's a risk I have felt comfortable with since I began writing about autism as a teenager because I am proud of my autistic identity and the work I have done within our community for what has been the majority of my life now.

You're hired!

You did it! You got the job offer! This is where things get kind of funky to integrate into the workplace and decide if this is truly a place you want to be. You might only have a certain amount of time to decide, so you'll want to iron out the details pretty quickly to know when your start date is, prepare for a new routine, and perhaps even negotiate your salary before accepting an offer.

- *You might want to negotiate before accepting an offer.* Not all employers give their best offer first. Have confidence and an idea of what salaries and opportunities for growth are standard within the company, industry, and its competitors.

- *After hiring might be when you want to talk about accommodations.* You might want to meet with your supervisor or human resources to discuss accommodations once you have an offer in hand to see if you can have your needs met, or you'll want to do this after accepting and as part of your new employee onboarding.

- *Review the benefits package.* This is something I might not have given a lot of thought to until I was working, but see what you're entitled to as an employee beyond your salary. Is training covered? Do you get health insurance? Retirement matching? How much time do you get off for vacations?

If everything looks good to you, accept the offer, know you're hired, and you are off to onboarding and getting ready to start working. Onboarding at a new job can be filling out paperwork, signing forms, necessary training, or a new hire orientation. For me, every first day of work was onboarding by just signing and reading policies and meeting everyone I would be working with. It is an exciting time to start a new career or job, and one of the biggest steps out there towards independence and showing that autistic people truly do belong everywhere.

Navigating the workplace— supervisors, colleagues, and more

Once you're hired and starting, it's up to you to navigate the new workplace culture. You'll probably be full of observations on the first day, and know that now your job, other than doing a good job, is keeping your job (if you do want to leave, you will want to leave on your own terms, not because your contract was terminated for poor behavior or performance). Ask and learn what the dress code is if you don't have a required uniform (every workplace I was at had different dress codes; some wore jeans on Fridays while others wore a suit every day or only when we had to see clients or go to court), but make sure you look neat, clean, and presentable each day.

This goes without saying, but treat everyone with respect. You do not have to be best friends with your colleagues or supervisors if you do not want to be. You might set explicit boundaries about how close work friends or after-work friends you want to be with your colleagues. For instance, you might not want to see people outside of work or work-related functions, or they might not want to see you, but you might be lunch buddies or friendly to each other within the office.

Harassment

A lot of autistic adults already have experience with bullying from childhood and adolescence. The findings on workplace bullying for autistic employees, however, are a bit more convoluted: a 2012 study reported one-third of autistic employees experienced bullying or harassment at work, while a 2009 report from the US Department of Education found more than 88 percent of young people with autism reported being treated "pretty well" at work (both cited in Hensel 2017). Bullying or harassment at work can be subtle. Social bullying and other forms of exclusion may be more prevalent if people do not understand the differences associated with autism. Social bullying at work can be exclusion, offhand comments, or public reprimands, but these do not rise to the level of harassment (Nagele-Piazza 2018). Exclusion at work and the occasional offhand comment can be hurtful, and you might want to talk it out with the colleague who is hurting you before taking it up with human resources or a supervisor.

But some of the difficulties that autistic employees face may border on harassment rather than social bullying. If you are being harassed, you might have legal recourse and should definitely document the incidents with human resources or supervisors and managers. Harassment on the basis of autism or disability is a form of discrimination. The US Equal Employment Opportunity Commission (EEOC)'s web page on disability discrimination explains that "although the law doesn't prohibit simple teasing, offhand comments, or isolated incidents that are not very serious, harassment is illegal when it is so frequent or severe that it creates a hostile or offensive work environment or when it results in an adverse employment decision (such as being fired or demoted)" (US EEOC n.d.). These instances of harassment and discrimination may invoke your rights under the Americans with Disabilities Act (ADA) (more on the ADA can be found under "Making My Mark on the World: Self-Advocacy").

Work events

Office events and retreats have the potential to be a lot of fun, but can also be really intimidating. When I first started at a law firm job, we had an overnight retreat in the Florida Keys: we spent the day sailing, kayaking, swimming, spending time on the beach, and exploring before settling down for a dinner all together and relaxing at the hotel. Some people drank a lot of alcohol while others did not. I had a wonderful time and saw my colleagues as fully human—though there was a persistent question at the back of my head about professionalism.

Probably one of the most intimidating aspects of work events is alcohol since it blurs the rules of professionalism and acting appropriately. Whether it is happy hour at a bar or restaurant or an out-of-town retreat, alcohol is often offered or encouraged. I do not drink primarily, so I either politely decline or set a limit on how much to drink (I used to watch *Millionaire Matchmaker* when it was on TV, and the matchmaker enforced a two-drink limit because that was enough alcohol for some people to feel socially brave but not appear sloppy). If you decline, do not feel pressured to accept or that you owe anyone an explanation for why you are not drinking because it is none of their business if it is a moral, medical, or personal decision.

No-dread networking

Confession: I hate traditional networking. It is one of the "adult" social and professional activities I truly do not always understand. I do not know how neurotypical people think the best place to hand out business cards and find mentorship is in a loud and crowded ballroom or restaurant, but sometimes the food is good. Networking can be particularly cumbersome for autistic people because there are a lot of unwritten social rules and unconventional norms, the situations can be a sensory onslaught, and the stakes can be high.

Chances are, you'll have to go to some kind of networking event in your life to advance your career or you had to do it in college, or you might go hoping to make new friends. Whatever your motivation, there are a few things to keep in mind in order to make it less intimidating and dreadful:

- *Figure out what you're taking with you and the logistics of going.* I like to have a few things in my purse or briefcase no matter what when I go to a networking or social event that is work-adjacent. Here is my must-have list of items and plans:

  - *How you are getting to and from the event.* I live in a major city without a car. Depending on the time of day, I do not feel safe taking commuter trains or other forms of public transport. If I am taking a rideshare, I like to calculate when I should leave my house or office, so I am on time (I do not want my entrance to be a spectacle). If you are going with a colleague or friend, make sure to coordinate what time you will be leaving together, who is driving, and how you are planning on getting home. Safety is first and foremost.

  - *Business cards.* I have had professional business cards

since I was 16 years old and wanted to direct people to my website to view my artwork. I designed them myself to have my artwork on the front and back, as well as my name, email, and website on one side. Since my late teens, my personal brand and professional identity have evolved. I have had cards printed on my behalf for specific occasions—when I served on nonprofit boards, I had special cards with the organization's name, address, and my title on them.

If you aren't sure how to get business cards or if your job didn't provide them (yet), you can always ask your supervisor when to expect them or order your own in bulk from a local printing vendor or a reputable products company like Vistaprint or Moo. They should have your name, job title, and contact information on them. For a bit of personal flair, I had my artwork alongside my last law firm's logo on one side of my business cards, and all of my information (name, job title, physical address of the office, email address, and phone number) on the other side. It was memorable and also true to me while giving the recipient all the necessary information to get in touch with me.

— *A snack.* In case the food isn't good, or you are on a limited diet or have sensory aversions to certain kinds of food, I recommend either having a snack before going to an event or taking one with you in your bag. Your stomach will thank you!

— *A coat, sweater, and/or blazer.* Depending on the dress code, it might be a professional event, and depending on the weather or location, it might be cold inside of the event. I live in Florida, so it never truly gets cold outside, but it can be chilly inside, so I will wear a professional-looking black or navy cardigan or blazer over my outfit to stay warm. Nothing worse than being cold. If it's cold outside, the place might also have a coat check, so don't worry about carrying your warm garments around with you the whole time.

- *Prepare a few scripts of what you might want to talk about.* You made it to the event. Another human who is not someone from your office is talking to you or introducing themselves. What do you even say? What are you supposed to do, other than be polite? People usually like to talk about themselves, so sometimes it might be best to let the other person lead and for you to ask questions if you find something particularly interesting, ask more questions about that thing, and have a conversation about it.

But if they're asking you questions, you might want to have a script or some canned answers, so you appear super-confident. Most companies and professionals talk about an "elevator pitch," or a 30-second to a minute version of who you are and what you do. It sounds intimidating to summarize the entire essence of your personal and professional identities, so I like to distill interactions into pieces.

I have a rough idea of how I would introduce myself to a new person and what body language I feel most comfortable with (some people are into handshakes or other touchy gestures), when I might hand them a business card (right away, so they know how to spell my name or can glance down if it is not on a nametag I'm wearing) or ask for theirs, and some questions I might want to ask them. Sometimes I'll ask what they do, why they find it interesting, and how long they've been doing that thing, or we'll have something in common like where we went to school or a special interest (this makes the conversation infinitely easier).

Having ideas of how to introduce yourself, excuse yourself, and speak about your professional interests are sure-fire ways to feel less awkward when you are in a situation filled with people you may not know very well.

Sometimes you know someone important to you might be at an event and you'd like to talk to them and be brave enough to strike up a conversation. I like to research these people and their work biographies (nothing too deep, like a personal Facebook account, but LinkedIn or their company bio are totally acceptable to peruse) before going to an event, so I have background information on them and a jumping-off point for conversation—maybe we both like dogs or have the same favorite football team. It makes you stand out, look confident, and you have a game plan to ease your anxieties.

- *Set reasonable goals or expectations for yourself.* As an attorney, I often go to networking events for legal societies. Working in the autism space, I also go to events with professionals and parents. Sometimes we go to events to have fun, meet new people, or get our names out there. Each situation is different, so I make sure I have a goal or expectation in mind because it can be overwhelming otherwise, and having a strategy makes me feel in control of an event beyond my control.

Ask yourself why you are planning to show up and keep that in mind. Sometimes, for me, that goal is to say hello to someone I have not seen in a while, make one new connection, eat some good food, or find a mentor.

If I have a feeling a situation can be overwhelming for any reason, I keep something more reasonable in mind: stay for an hour. An hour is enough time for me to shake a few hands and hold a few small-talk conversations. If I am tired, don't meet anyone or have any meaningful conversations, or feel overwhelmed after an hour, I feel

comfortable leaving and will give myself credit for showing up and putting myself out there.

- *Attend with someone you know so you will not be alone and have a teammate.* You might not go alone to an event for work because your boss or a colleague is also going with you, or someone else you know is driving you to and from the event. Either way, going with a trusted ally can be helpful for more than just logistics, especially if that ally is outgoing and socially savvy. That someone can help introduce you to new people and build you up. It always sounds better when someone else says nice things about you than if you try to say nice things about yourself (it is much more impactful if someone else says that "Haley is a great writer" than if I tell you myself "I'm a great writer").

  If I'm going to a professional or social event by myself, I try to be in situations where I will be likely to have an acquaintance or at least something in common with others there.

  If I have a trusted ally in attendance (especially if they are reliable transport), I also feel better knowing this is someone I can let know what my backup plan is if an event is overwhelming, unsafe, or uncomfortable for me.

- *Have a backup plan if the event is overwhelming.* Traditional networking events can be really difficult to navigate: the venues are often loud and crowded, and there are plenty of unwritten social rules and expectations. Sometimes alcohol served at events might create pressure if you are someone who chooses not to drink; whatever the reason, organizers, acquaintances, friends, and colleagues alike should respect any decision you make concerning what you eat or drink.

  Group meetups like networking events can be overwhelming because of the societal expectations of eye
  contact and prescribed conversation rules, the noise and

crowds, or other situational factors. To regain control of the situation, setting some personal boundaries and exit strategies can help.

If you're on a planning committee or in contact with the event organizers, consider suggesting that a larger space or setting can have a designated quiet space or area to reorganize thoughts and regain composure. While I have never seen a quiet space or sensory room at networking events or receptions outside of autism conferences, they are far more welcoming than leaving the building or hiding out in the restrooms in order to catch your breath.

If an event is too much, have an exit strategy so you can leave safely and not make a scene. You can be polite and thank the hosts, wrap up any remaining conversations without being too abrasive ("Meeting you tonight was lovely, but unfortunately, I have to get home to my cat" or something along those lines always works well), and you can mention you will see people again soon or reach out via email or another means (you did get their business card, right?). Then you can dash out, go home, and take care of yourself.

- *Get creative and use online networking tools.* One of the things about autistic people that always makes me continue to admire us is how resourceful and creative we are. Networking doesn't just mean cocktail parties, work events, or in-person gatherings. You can connect with new people in your chosen career or industry or make new friends with similar interests through the internet. One of my autistic colleagues met me—and countless other law students and lawyers—through LinkedIn and Facebook, often finding our profiles and writing a nice (and possibly scripted) introduction on the social media messaging platforms, or via email.

MONEY MATTERS: RESPONSIBILITY AND NOT GOING BROKE

In the quest for independence, autistic people often recognize the importance of financial understanding, and may feel frustrated at their lack of financial savviness or money management skill set. Autistic young people shared with researchers that (1) managing finances was a key part of their definition of independence; (2) they worried about their lack of money management skills; and (3) that poor financial skills were a barrier to independence (Cheak-Zamora *et al.* 2017).

Finance is a very scary concept as a young autistic adult, especially if you're not too aware of the world around you and how much things cost. We are also very generous and caring towards those we love. There is nothing I wouldn't do for those I love or care about, including buying them gifts. Or we want to invest in our special interests with abandon because they just...make us that happy. Some of us have rent, student loans, debt, and other financial obligations. Some of us are trying to save for our futures. Since the decisions we make as young people impact the rest of our lives, it's important to keep in mind how getting your finances in order and practicing fiscal responsibility now can help you later on.

Opening a bank account

One of the first things you will want to do as an adult is open a bank account. There are two main types of personal bank accounts: checking (current) and savings accounts. Checking accounts are typically used for everyday transactions, like depositing and withdrawing money, buying things on a debit card, and paying bills. They do not always earn interest. Savings accounts, however, are better for saving money, building an emergency fund, and earning interest, but you might have to have a minimum balance or be unable to withdraw money without paying a fee.

To open an account, either go in person to the bank branch of your choice or visit their website to open an account online. When deciding on a financial institution, think about which banks have low minimum balances or monthly fees, have conveniently located branches and ATMs near where you live, work, or travel (it does not cost you anything to use your bank's ATM machines, but other banks or independent ATMs may charge you transaction fees), or that also have attractive credit card offers (banks are more likely to approve their own customers for their branded credit cards). I also like that my bank has an easy-to-use mobile app so I can check my balances, deposits, and credit cards all in one place—if you're technologically savvy or inclined, this might be worth considering too.

When you decide on a bank, make an appointment or walk in and speak to an advisor or bank teller or begin the process online. I always went in person, so a human could answer any questions I had. It can be overwhelming to hear about the different options, but a professional or support person can easily help you. You need to have government ID like a state-issued ID card or driver's license and information like your Social Security Number or Taxpayer Identification Number, date of birth, and depending on the bank, a cash or check to make a minimum initial deposit with.

When you open a checking account, you will also get a checkbook. Make sure you store this in a safe place so people can't write checks in your name and steal your money. Checkbooks also have a little ledger in them to keep track of the check numbers, who the check was made out to, and how much money it was for.

Opening a business account if you are self-employed

If you are a small business owner or self-employed, you will want to open a business bank account to separate your income from your personal assets (it helps keep things organized). To open a business bank account in the US, you need the same information you'd need for a personal account, but you should also have an Employer Identification Number (EIN) or proof of incorporation, and a form of government ID. To get an EIN, which is a number used for taxes (if you are an individual or sole proprietor, you can use this instead of your Social Security Number for privacy and safety purposes), apply for one through the IRS online and you will get approved nearly instantly.

I would definitely go to a bank branch in person for this since I found opening a business account much more overwhelming in terms of information provided than when I opened personal accounts, and my bank had specific advisors just for small business owners and contractors.

Budgeting

Something autistic people might struggle with is realizing just how fast we spend money, keeping track of it, and thinking because we put it on a credit or debit card, it is somehow not as real as cash money. One of the most crucial skills to help keep your spending in line and to make sure you don't go too deep into debt or can't keep up with your obligations is to set up a budget and to stick to it. If anything, it is yet another routine, except it requires a bit more careful planning to execute.

- *Make sure to budget and pay for the important things first.* Your biggest priorities should be the things you need in order to live. Rent, utilities, and food should be your top priorities. Same with healthcare, if you are paying for that. If you have and drive a car to work, your car payment and gas are also up there on important things to pay for first. When creating a budget, determine how much each of these things costs you per month, and be sure to set aside money to pay those bills.

If something like food is costing more than you budget for, take a look at your spending habits. Restaurants and ordering beverages are some of the sneakiest expenses in a food-related budget. Declining to order coffee, tea, soda, or alcohol, or choosing to go out to eat less frequently can save you money. It is almost always more cost-effective to buy groceries, cook, and eat at home or bring food to the office than it is to go to restaurants. This is especially something to think about if you have a job and like to go out to lunch with your colleagues and are expected to pay for your meal. It becomes more effective to either go out less, order less expensive food (and always order water), or bring your own food to work.

- *Look for the little things that add up to a lot of expense.* One of my closest friends regularly complains about having no money, but she faithfully goes to a coffee shop for coffee at least once a day. While I do not know the exact details of her financial history, her coffee habit is one of those little things that might not seem like much, but quickly puts a huge damper on budgeting, saving, and having money for more pressing things like her rent, food, or car payment. With some quick estimations, I figured out grabbing one coffee or tea at the local cafe could easily be a $5/day habit that quickly spirals into $150 a month (I assumed $5/day for 30 days). If you drank a $5 coffee every single day for a year, that's $1800 (in some major cities, that is an entire month's worth of rent!). Even a simple cut or reducing a seemingly inexpensive habit down to a few days a week can make it so you are able to prioritize or save money.

- *Saving money.* You might choose to put a portion of your budget or paychecks from working into a savings account. Try to save $20 per paycheck; it'll add up by the end of the year. You could also think about cutting the coffee habit we talked about earlier (if you saved your "coffee money" each day, you'd quickly contribute $150 per month to your savings). Saving is a good idea so you will always have cash on hand for an emergency, like a hospital visit, an unexpected car repair, losing your job, or another unforeseeable event, without being on the brink of financial ruin. Financial advisors recommend having a few months' salary put away, but if you aren't working or have a relatively low cost of living, a few hundred dollars might be enough for this "emergency expense" fund.

  Other savings might be going towards a greater financial goal, like owning a home. Or something less exciting, like paying taxes if your tax liability isn't deducted out of your paychecks regularly. You can always talk to a financial advisor, accountant, or other tax advisor for your specific situation here.

- *Using budgeting tools.* One of the highest recommended budget tools out there is Mint, which can help you manage your entire financial life at once—it shows you how much money you have in your account(s), what your spending habits are, your credit score, and how to create a budget. I like the easy-to-use interface and reminders, and it's free.

I'm not even 25 and you want me to save for retirement?

When you're a young person, the last thing you're thinking about is who you will be and how much money you will need and want when you are in your sixties and beyond. Needless to say, retirement matching, 401(k) (retirement) plans, and the idea of putting money into savings or investment funds all seems overwhelming, especially when you're hoping not to be financially dependent on someone else.

The idea of retirement or retirement benefits surely did not occur to me when I first graduated from school and entered the workforce. It wasn't until I received a collection of different tax documents in the mail that I had to even consider such things. In late 2019 and early 2020, it seemed a new 1099 (tax) form arrived each day, and then I received a W-2 (tax) form from the full-time job I had recently left. I owed quite a bit in taxes, and then my accountant explained to me how contributing to a retirement fund could be tax deductions that would help me later on and mean I would be buying into that instead of writing a check to the IRS. It felt like the most adult thing I ever did. I was suddenly 25 with a retirement account.

Depending on what your financial advisor has in mind, saving for retirement early on can pay off in the long run and/ or save you money today. When I'm in my later life, I'll have an investment or retirement fund I can use, and I'll certainly be thanking my past self for thinking ahead.

Don't lose the plastic: credit and debit cards

I was about to go off to college when my dad and I went to a branch of a bank to set up a student checking account for me to use. One of the things that came with a new bank account was a debit card, or ATM card, so I could put purchases on it or withdraw money out of the account either by going to the bank or using an ATM machine. It was a pretty empowering moment, as was every other bank account I opened as well for business, savings, or checking—both for myself and as a business owner. Sure, the easiest thing to tell you is...don't lose your credit and debit cards and keep them in a safe place, but there are many lessons to be learned in the realm of financial literacy when it comes to the little pieces of plastic that allow you to make purchases or withdraw money.

Credit cards

I often think of the premises of the movie *Confessions of a Shopaholic* when it comes down to credit cards. The main character is a little girl who, early on in the movie, admires adult women buying beautiful clothes by swiping what she believes are "magic cards." Fast forward to when she is an adult, and she is knee-deep in credit card debt surrounded by beautiful clothes and shoes, attempting to figure out how to pay the debt down. Her money problems cause her to become a habitual liar, causing rifts in her relationships with a love interest and her best friend/roommate. She thankfully gets her debt situation under control by ultimately selling off her beloved clothes and ends up with the guy, but the movie feels like a cautionary tale of sorts—especially since it is easy to get caught up in the "I'll pay for this later" or "it isn't real money until the bill comes" mentality.

Credit cards operate under the premise of allowing consumers to make purchases on "credit," meaning the loaner or credit card company trusts them to pay back the money later, when the bill is due each month. If the bill is not paid in full or on time, credit card companies charge interest—an extra percentage on the balance you owe (this is how they make money, betting you will not pay your balance in full each and every month). Depending on the card, interest can be as high as about 25 percent. Credit card debt is a large contributor to debt nationwide, and the average American household in 2019 carried about $8398 in credit card debt (Debt.org 2021). Most cardholders have multiple cards to spread across so they don't hit their credit limits, but this is a quick way to allow your debt and spending to spiral out of control.

Credit cards are not inherently bad. If you use them responsibly, it is a great way to build credit so you can eventually secure a loan for a business, a house, or something else major—a lot of banks do not lend to people with poor credit or a limited credit history. Most credit cards also have cool rewards programs based on your spending habits by giving you points that can be spent on travel or gift cards, or cash to apply to your monthly statements.

Credit cards come with a lot of responsibility since you keep taking on an increased debt load from interest rates and they require you to track your spending meticulously. Here are some ways to manage them:

- *Treat it like a debit card.* Meaning, only spend money you have. With debit cards, you can't spend more than your balance in your checking account. If you pretend a credit card works exactly the same way, you can pay your bill in full each month, build credit, and not get charged the monthly interest rate. If you are just building credit, make small purchases on the card so you can practice paying it each month.

- *Or treat it as an emergency money thing for large purchases to be financed.* You might not have cash on hand to finance a major car repair, but you can put it on a credit card and pay it out over time. Keep in mind that it might cost you more this way, but if you don't have the money at the moment, a credit card can keep you from having to ask family or another person or bank to loan you money.

- *You will want to pay your credit card(s) on time.* If you miss payments, you will get charged a late fee each month. To avoid this, try to at least make the minimum monthly payment (it's usually pretty low, like $25 or so). Sure, you'll get charged interest on your remaining balance, but a late fee is extra money you won't want to pay.

- *Pay your credit cards in full if possible.* This is the easiest way to avoid credit card debt, and easiest to do if you treat the credit card like a debit card. Each credit card has a low minimum monthly payment amount, but the company charges interest on the unpaid balance; depending on your card, that might be as low as zero interest (through an introductory offer) or as high as 25 percent. That is how credit card companies make money. If you pay your balance in full, you are not in debt and it also increases your creditworthiness to other lenders, such as when you need credit or a loan to buy or lease a car or get approved for a mortgage on a house.

- *Check your monthly statement meticulously for overcharges or unexplained charges.* I buy a lot of stuff. I am admittedly someone who shops for clothes for fun. I always check when things are overcharged and try to keep track of what I buy and if I return something, when the refunds post. By virtue of online shopping and using cards at different places, you can end up with charges on purchases you didn't make because of identity theft. Identity theft happens through people stealing your credit card information. Thieves obtain your credit card information through hacking or skimming devices. There might be transactions you did not make on your statement, so you should read your itemized statement carefully each month and keep records of your credit card purchases. If you see anything that looks fishy or that you did not authorize, you can dispute the charge with the credit card company if you catch it within a certain time frame (usually 60 days or so). You won't have to pay it, and your credit card company might freeze your card to avoid any new charges coming through, or they will cancel the current card and mail you a new one for your protection.

This is also a great time to look over monthly subscriptions—often one of the biggest culprits of unexplained charges. If you sign up for a lot of free trials, you might see charges for subscriptions you did not cancel. While you might not be able to dispute those charges, going through your statements can sometimes be a rude awakening and reminder to executive function well enough one day to cancel those subscriptions to magazines, massage places, Netflix, or whatever it may be that you aren't using in order to save money and keep costs down.

Bills and avoiding debt

I am pretty sure the absolute worst day of the month is when the financial statements come in the mail to tell me what my account balances are and how much I owe. Those days suddenly make everything real.

One of the biggest struggles with paying bills shouldn't be having the funds to pay them (if you followed some of the earlier tips, you should've budgeted for this)—but actually remembering to pay on time to avoid nasty letters, collections agents, or pesky interest charges and late fees. This can be difficult for anyone, but for autistic people, the executive functioning difficulties can make this so much more difficult.

- *Prioritize all of the different bills you have to pay.* This is the best way to figure out what is important and to stay out of debt or avoid an unmanageable debt load. What are the things that are by far the most important that must be paid every month, without fail? Or what are the number one things that will have sudden and severe consequences for you (and possibly your partner or other family members in your household) if they're not taken care of and paid for immediately? The National Consumer Law Center's *Surviving Debt* handbook (2020) says the highest priority debts are rent, utilities like electric and water, car leases, court and justice system debts (these can be as small as traffic tickets), and if you have kids and are divorced or not with the other parent, child support obligations (you could go to prison for avoiding child support payments).

Your "second priority" bills might be very important with fewer immediate consequences. They won't evict you or switch your lights off if you are short or missed a payment because your budget did not shake out properly, but can wreck your future if they are delayed for too long. These "higher priority" bills, according to the National Consumer Law Center, are federal student loans, mortgage payments if you own a home, and property and federal tax obligations.

The next group of bills are those that can also spiral out of control if not managed or can be a complete pain in your side. The National Consumer Law Center says these are lower priority because you won't immediately be sued for nonpayment or have money or property taken from you. These obligations include unexpected home repairs and maintenance, medical bills, credit cards, and private student loans.

In order to stay out of trouble, and with that list in mind, you can budget accordingly and also know to always start with the top priority stuff like your rent, electricity, and court/legal-related judgment matters before delving into some of the other more pressing concerns.

- *Set up autopay on bills.* Certain bills, like my cable and internet, I would never remember to pay if I did not have it automatically set up to send money to the provider or charged monthly on a credit or debit card. I also have autopay on subscriptions that I use, like for Netflix, gym memberships, or news media. Based on the priority of bills, a lot of autopay things are low priority, with the exception of health insurance, because losing coverage could be catastrophic. Be sure to check when subscriptions renew and how often they are billed in case there is a dispute or discrepancy between what you are paying and what you owe, and so you know how often you are paying.

- *Set calendar reminders.* On my calendar, I keep reminders recurring every month for the days I get billed for subscriptions like Netflix and my gym membership as well as rent due dates and when my credit card statement closes each month and when the payment is due. That way, I know when to expect the charges to come through for recurring billing charges and when my major bills are due. Even though some of those are on autopay, I still keep them on my calendar so I stay accountable and know what's to come.

- *Make a list of all the charges to figure out how much money to send in for payment.* I do this with credit cards, especially since I will be looking for disputed charges or pending refunds or temporary authorizations. That way, I avoid overpaying if I am going to do my best to pay a statement balance in full.

Making My Mark on the World: Self-Advocacy

Self-advocacy is a form of independence and empowerment that we talk about—a lot. But what is self-advocacy after all? Self-advocacy is a skill set we use to make our own decisions and speak up for ourselves. It is also a political movement for people with disabilities. To sum it up, "self-advocacy—as a personal and political philosophy—is a movement primarily of and by [people with disabilities] who are making their own decisions, speaking for themselves and for others with disabilities, and taking control over their lives" (The Minnesota Governor's Council on Developmental Disabilities 2021). The self-advocacy movement began within the intellectual disability community and evolved to be further inclusive of autism and neurodiversity throughout time.

There is one huge myth in advocacy, that being an "advocate" is meant for professionals, like lawyers, policymakers, politicians, or lobbyists. Being an advocate or a self-advocate does not require a title, though some autistic self-advocates do go on to be fantastic lobbyists and policy advocates, like those serving on state developmental disability councils, or folks like my friend Conner Cummings, who, along with his mom, lobbied state legislators in Virginia to pass Conner's Law, requiring financial support from parents to help adult children with disabilities. Along with his mom, Conner is looking to close the loophole in child support laws to provide financial assistance so autistic children continue to receive parental support once they reach adulthood.

Ultimately, self-advocacy is a form of communication above all else. We self-advocate every day, multiple times a day, whenever we make decisions and speak up for ourselves at home, at work, with our families and friends, in our romantic relationships, or even when we decide what we would like to eat at a restaurant. Basically, all of us are self-advocates. I am not more of a self-advocate because I have a license to practice law. Any time we use our own voices, with or without assistance, to get what we need to succeed, we are practicing self-advocacy.

Self-advocacy does not discriminate based on the level of support needs an autistic person has or how they communicate. Whether or not you speak verbally, type to communicate, or use gestures or assistive technology, you deserve to have your voice heard as well as your preferences and boundaries respected and honored. These skills help us all maintain a level of independence and to express what's on our minds.

For more information on self-advocacy, the People First movement internationally, the Autistic Self Advocacy Network (ASAN), and Self Advocates Becoming Empowered (SABE) all have resources on self-advocacy and are primarily led by self-advocates.

BEING AN EFFECTIVE SELF-ADVOCATE

Most people do not know or recognize the vastness of the disability rights movement and the branches of disability justice, self-advocacy, and independent living movements. Often, disability history and culture are overlooked and ignored in history and teaching. If our roots in self-advocacy are unexplored, how is it that we can ever become empowered and effective self-advocates?

Earlier in life, allies have the potential to pave the way or us to feel comfortable speaking up and making decisions for ourselves. One of the most surprising things neurotypical parents hear me say about their younger children in particular is to teach them self-advocacy skills at a young age. School does not teach self-advocacy; the tradition begins at home. Sometimes it is as simple as asking what a child would like to eat for dinner that night.

I typically advise parents that one of the easiest ways to welcome the conversation is to include the child in their meetings at school in regard to their Individual Education Plan (IEP). Students with disabilities who receive special education services have an IEP, a collection of documents put together with input from the student's family, teachers, and other support professionals to help determine the student's goals and measure success. However, it is too rare that the student is included in their own IEP meetings, so if they are able to participate or share their goals, they should be there.

While I did not go to public school at a young age, my parents set up annual meetings with my teachers before school began, where they would plan my goals and let them get to know a bit about me ahead of the first day of classes. When I knew I was autistic, I would join these meetings and I got to share some of my goals. The earliest goal I remember sharing at age nine is that I wanted to be friends with more girls. My teacher made a more intentional effort to help me make friends with girls. It made me feel empowered. The older I was, the more involved I would be in these meetings, ultimately giving me the tools to advocate for myself (with guidance, because I always like to ask for advice on tough situations) throughout college, law school, the workplace, and other life situations.

When we are adults, our parents can't always be our initial

advocates. Sometimes, at best, they can advocate *with* us, but not always *for* us. The same goes for romantic partners, friends, teachers, support people, caregivers, and other relatives. Again, being a self-advocate is all about communication in addition to a little bit of confidence and empowerment rather than a learned helplessness.

To gain some self-advocacy skills, it is best to reflect on how you share messages with other people. How do you best communicate your thoughts and ideas? Are you a more effective writer than a talker? Are your ideas clearer when you use assistive technology or gestures? With that in mind, think about what your goal is. What is it that you need or want others to do or help you with? You can rank these desires and needs in order of importance; sometimes it is as difficult as creating access, and other times it is as simple as asking others to use quieter voices to avoid a sensory overload. Then, consider putting it all together so the people in your life can help you. Being a stronger communicator and self-advocate helps you make decisions rather than have someone else make decisions on your behalf.

If talking to others makes you nervous, that is totally okay. Self-advocacy is a skill set that takes practice. Try to rehearse with someone who understands or in front of the mirror. Make a list of bullet points. Edit and reread what you wrote. Do what you have to do so you feel comfortable making a request or demand or sharing how you feel about a situation or decision.

USING YOUR SELF-ADVOCACY SKILLS FOR GOOD: COMMUNITY ENGAGEMENT

Now that you are a pretty strong self-advocate and self-assured adult, you can use self-advocacy and leadership skills for a purpose bigger than just yourself. After all, the self-advocacy *movement* encourages us to speak for ourselves *and* on behalf of others with disabilities. There are a lot of ways to advocate for ourselves on a larger scale and become more involved in the communities we live and work in. Sure, I began developing self-advocacy skills as a young person asking for things at home and standing up for myself. I began speaking about autism when I was 13 and was invited to be a panelist at the Autism Society of America annual conference, and grew my interests in autistic advocacy alongside law and policy from there. But being part of the community beyond myself was a value set instilled in me from a young age, beginning with donating toys and clothes to folks in need and being called on to advise others when I volunteered at a local nonprofit in high school. Community engagement has been formative to my growth as a person since I was a child.

One of the beautiful things about adulthood is that we are constantly improving and discovering new things about ourselves. Even when we are done with school, we are still learning. I am a proud lifelong learner. Some of the best learning I have ever done is outside of classrooms, when I learned from other people and their experiences. As adult humans, we have responsibilities in our own lives, but also to each other. This section is all about those ways we can be better people to ourselves, the world around us, and the communities we are a part of it. We can give back by donating our time, become politically and civically involved, learn about people who are different than us, and recognize the power we hold (and give it to people who historically don't have power). As people, we also have another responsibility: to stay out of trouble and to use our powers of self-advocacy and independence for good.

Volunteering

I grew up being told the importance of giving back to others. I have always wanted to help others however possible. When I couldn't give money, I realized I could give my time through direct action or serving on a committee or board, so I did that instead. Ultimately, the most valuable resource we have is time. And giving your time and effort can mean a lot of different things; for my mom, it meant dipping hundreds of pretzels in chocolate to put in gift baskets for a fundraiser and then curating what went in to each basket. For me, it means providing input on a board right now, but when I was in college, it meant hanging out with autistic kids on weekends at public parks to provide respite to parents who were overwhelmed between work and family responsibilities. A couple of times, I created original artwork to be used on t-shirts for an organization to sell. Sometimes volunteering meant working a check-in booth at an event and handing out nametags. Volunteerism means different things to different people, and each of us has a valuable talent, skill, or time to share with our communities.

Where do you start if you want to volunteer? The best way to get involved is finding something you care about and would like to give time to without expecting money or prestige in return. Maybe it's your city's annual anime convention, helping to plan a 5K run or walk for charity (or signing up to run or walk it for a good cause!), joining a group for a beach or park cleanup to have a cleaner environment, helping a political campaign, or giving back to children in your community. A great place to build on volunteer experience is finding something in line with your special interests or passions, or even building on a future career choice.

Advisory board participation

The first time I was asked to serve on a nonprofit board of directors or an advisory board that wasn't a student organization at school I was a senior in college. I would be one of many voices who would be reading reports and attending meetings a few times a year to help make major decisions for a school for high school-aged students with disabilities that would help prepare them for the workforce and teach employment skills along with regular postsecondary curriculum requirements. While I did not go to a specialized program like that—I was just an autistic college senior double majoring in psychology and criminology with sights set on law school—I would be the only disabled or autistic voice at the table. I realized at that table that my voice mattered alongside nonprofit donors, educators, parents, and other stakeholders because I had more first-person insight into how the students may be feeling or what they may be experiencing. We reviewed the school's finances, curriculum, fundraising efforts, and available scholarship opportunities, and were able to ask the important questions. It was invaluable to see the ins and outs of how an organization functioned.

I served as that board's secretary at one point, before my term ended. Since then, I have served or currently serve on several other nonprofit or professional organization boards, or advisory boards, to help guide the organization's mission, fundraising (again, as a young person, donating money might not be on the cards for you, but driving a strategy to help them bring in money might be), or to hold them accountable.

Advisory boards exist in numerous capacities, especially within the autism community. They help guide policy and research priorities for autistic people and their families or are a part of nonprofit organizations (largely led by neurotypicals) to ensure they have input from autistic constituents as well. Volunteering on a board of directors or advisory board can benefit both you and the organization.

What boards do and why join a board

Board members are (typically unpaid) volunteers who give their time to help guide an organization's leadership, fundraising, programs, initiatives, and operational strategies.

Board members are also able to hold employees and the rest of the board accountable in some way. For me, I have always come from the perspective that volunteering is important, and serving on the board of an organization is basically being a volunteer leader. I am also an early-career professional who does not always have money to donate across multiple causes and places I care for.

I often advise autistic adults looking to get involved away from autistic communities online to seek out their local autism organizations. Lots of autistic adults are frustrated with a lack of representation, a focus on neurotypical family members, or cure-oriented nonprofit missions, and often do not know where to turn in order to help change that. Shouting into the void on the internet does not typically incentivize community change. But chances are, local and national nonprofit boards (much like those in my community) are often lacking autistic and disabled voices. At the same time, it is important to make sure you are not volunteering or offering yourself up as a token. Each time I agree to serve either a one- or two-year term, I regularly find if I am the only autistic person at the meetings that I am pushing to add more autistic board members, especially folks who have different life experiences than I do (autistics who are older than me, or who are not the same gender, religion, sexual orientation, race, or are otherwise disabled). Chances are, you might be able to add more diversity or be a vocal advocate, learn how your community is served, lend your input at the highest level, and make some real change. One of my biggest victories was the first time a board I served on unanimously voted to install more autistic advocates onto the board after I insisted that we needed more than two self-advocates representing our local community.

I also learned a lot of valuable leadership skills serving, so you get what you put in. I learned to be less afraid to ask questions, since every board I have ever served on is related to an issue I care about in some way, which is often autism or disability related. This confidence carried over into other aspects of my life, including in law practice, where I am more inclined to ask insightful questions of clients, legal initiatives, or supervisors.

If you want to serve, or are considering serving, here are some things to look for or to ask about:

- *How long is the term you might be serving?* Board members serve annual terms depending on the organization's bylaws. I like to look for one- or two-year terms if I am adding new commitments, and then I can decide whether or not I want to do it again if there are term limits (or not). It is easier to stay until the end of the term than to resign, unless you feel resigning is paramount because your goals no longer match the organization's, or you truly do not have the time to serve.

- *What is the time commitment? Each week? Each month? Each year?* As a board member, you are usually expected to attend the regular board meetings at a minimum. Depending on the organization, these meetings might be as frequently as once per month, or as infrequently as once or twice a year. Most boards I served on meet every quarter, so they meet four times per year. If you serve in an executive leadership position (president, vice-president, secretary, or treasurer), you might have to go to extra meetings. If you are leading a project or serving on a subcommittee, you will probably be dedicating a few extra hours to a project or effort as well, so keep that in mind. One board I serve on requires that I am regularly in touch with a social media coordinator whenever the other members have something to share, so sometimes that is an hour each week in addition to regular meetings and subcommittee meetings. Again, keep in mind how much time you are willing to give, since chances are, you also have hobbies, family obligations, a job, or other things you would like to do in your free time.

- *Who else is on the board or in the organization?* Most organizations have the members of their board of directors featured on their website, so you can get a feel for who might be your new friends and colleagues in service. Most of them, like you, are not employees of the nonprofit or organization—they are there because they want to be. If you are on the fence about joining or want a less biased person to ask questions of, reach out to current board members and try to pick their brains a little—any time anyone has ever done this to me, I've been pretty open about my experiences.

  Checking out the composition of the board can also give you clues as to what an organization's priorities are—and provide valuable questioning fodder if you want to ask why you're being considered or you are asking yourself why you are getting involved. Representation matters, especially in autism-related causes. Are there a lot of self-advocates, or none at all? Is the board racially diverse? Are there women, trans, and nonbinary people? Are all of the board members retirees with nothing better to do? These are questions to answer at the back of your mind, and see how that fits into what you're hoping to do and if it would be a group of people you'd feel comfortable working with or at least sitting through semi-regular meetings with for a few hours at a time.

- *What would you like to contribute?* This is the big one for me, since no organization, no matter how much I love it, is perfect. Am I lending my opinion as an autistic person, or do I want to just help improve the public relations effort? Sometimes, you might just be trying to grow as a leader and not know what you'd like to contribute. This is a question you might let percolate in your mind and have an answer evolving as time goes on.

- *What would you like to get out of the experience?* These

questions will help determine if volunteering in this way is too demanding on your mind or schedule, or if you feel it is a fit because of representation or a lack of representation. Asking what you want to give and get out of the experience is a great way to be honest with yourself too: maybe you want to give back or build something new, or you want to network more within the community. Asking questions of other board members or leaders and of yourself will help you determine what the best way to serve your community might be.

Power, privilege, and learning when to listen

Social justice education is probably one of the things I wished I had earlier in life. I was fortunate to attend a private high school, but it didn't teach its students about civil rights and social justice or how to be better allies and recognize how lucky they were that their parents could send them there—and to go out and do good in the world. I did not get my first taste of comprehensive social justice education until college, on a multicultural and diversity affairs weekend retreat. It was one of the most overwhelming weekends of my life—I was learning so much, but I couldn't wait to go back to my dorm because we were living in these camp bunks inside of cabins, and spending time without technology, people I knew and food I liked to eat, and I was scared to use the camp cabin showers because of the perceived lack of privacy. For an entire weekend, 50 students learned about what social justice was, what oppression, privilege, and marginalization were, how those concepts affected different groups, and how to be an ally to people facing systemic barriers to access. On the last day, we learned about disability and ableism; the morning began with a simulation where we were blindfolded or had earplugs or weren't able to use our hands during breakfast, to try to be more empathetic towards disabled folks. I eventually felt comfortable talking about my autism and my experience as a disabled person (I was the only person who identified as disabled on the retreat that weekend)—and it opened the floodgates for me to be a more vocal advocate about things that mattered rather than seeing myself and others as needy or overcoming autism and disability. It also helped me understand how my experiences are connected to others who are also sidelined in society because of who they are, and to spend more time listening. I only spoke on the last day of the retreat.

It has been over seven years since that introduction to social justice. Since then, one of the biggest lessons I have learned in any community activism or civic engagement is learning when to listen rather than speak. While your input is super-valuable, it is really crucial to learn and not to speak over people who might have different experiences than you. While as autistic people our voices often go silenced or unheard, there are other people who are also silenced or unheard. Those people are often multiply marginalized by, among other things, race, gender, religion, sexual orientation, where they are from, or socioeconomic status.

Talking about marginalization, especially in community activism and volunteer spaces, requires a bit of a primer on power and privilege. According to the social justice primer from Dartmouth College (n.d.), *power* is wielding influence along with the ability to make decisions that impact others. *Privilege* refers to advantages and benefits that individuals receive because of social groups they are perceived to be a part of, often at the expense or marginalization of another group. Who do you think holds power? People who are members of social groups with privilege—people who are (or pass as) white, able-bodied, Christian, men, English speaking, and/or heterosexual, and are in a good financial situation. You can experience privilege in some areas—like your perceived or actual racial and ethnic identity—and oppression and marginalization in others—like disability status and gender. In social justice initiatives, where we try to help and advocate on our behalf as well as others, it is an important step to take to recognize the ways in which we benefit from society's current structure, and the ways society puts up barriers to us. As autistic people, we are all marginalized by disability status—people will stereotype, discriminate, and treat us negatively because of our autism. We might be further marginalized by disability if we have a co-occurring mental or physical disability.

While most readers might identify as autistic, neurodivergent, or disabled, keep in mind that not all of us are solely marginalized on disability alone. It is not a single-issue identity or diversity issue. People can also experience negative treatment as a result of the color of their skin, gender identity, who they love, where they are from, and other disabilities. These things also influence someone's experience with being autistic—women and gender minorities are often diagnosed later than autistic boys and men, and autistic people of color face further discrimination in healthcare, diagnosis, and interactions with the police and the criminal justice system. Being from other parts of the world also impacts how a culture might look at autism. Your experience is inherently different than mine.

As a podcast host and volunteer, I get to interview different folks from within the autistic and autism communities each time we record. While we often have very lively and fun conversations, sometimes they take a turn towards the solemn and serious. My co-host and I do not want to speak over a guest since the interview is their time to shine, and we have an unspoken "shut up and listen" policy. Both of us are white women who graduated from law school—I am autistic; she is neurotypical. Neither of us wants to shout over or inadvertently de-platform the voice of someone who is nonbinary, trans, queer, practices a different religion, is a person of color, or has identities we might not share. If anything, we should be passing the mic to uplift voices, especially if someone is a member of a historically oppressed or currently underrepresented group (as often seen by conversations like #DisabilityTooWhite).

While we aim to understand, we will never have the same first-hand experience—we aim to pass the mic and uplift our siblings with different experiences and allow ourselves the opportunity to learn from them to be more inclusive and accepting humans.

Leading at work

You might not want to be a leader or activist in the nonprofit, political, or community sphere, but you might choose to take on different roles in the workplace to keep growing your career, through, for example, professional associations and employee resource groups. Thinking about your autistic and neurodivergent identity, you might also want to feel supported as you grow and pay it forward to make the road a bit smoother for the next group of neurodivergent job seekers, colleagues, employees, and clients.

I have always been the type to seek out leadership roles, whether at school or at work. I always felt that as a person with a disability, I had the potential to make a difference for the next group of folks. I also felt at times that being involved was part of proving my competence and talent—since so little would be expected of autistic and disabled employees, at first, I felt I had to go above and beyond to prove I belonged. As I learned in an implicit bias training not too long ago, marginalized workers "have to prove their competence while others have the presumption of competence." In competitive industries like law, disability is wrongly perceived as a weakness and something to be overcome, rather than one of my greatest strengths. Industries and individual workplaces have the ability to change to be more welcoming and inclusive, and you can play a role in making it better while also growing your career and your own relationship skills.

Depending on your industry, there are probably professional associations made up of people on the same path as you. For lawyers, these are called bar associations—collectives of lawyers that share a similar identity (I'm a member of my local women lawyers' association). They are dedicated to growing as professionals and provide mentoring and networking opportunities, lobbying efforts, and educational training. Through my involvement with statewide and local bar associations, I was able to meet lawyers in different areas in practice, bring the concerns of lawyers with disabilities and accessibility to the forefront, and learn new things from my colleagues. Most industries have a trade or affinity group or organization at national or state level. They may be unions, more social in nature, or associations for like-minded pros. It is a great way to network and grow—join, and if you feel good about it, you can take on a role to innovate within. After my first year of practice, I took on a role for my statewide bar association for young attorneys under the age of 36, and it has been a wonderful opportunity.

If you work for a large company, they might have what's known as employee resource groups, or affinity groups. Employee resource groups are led by employees who join forces around a shared characteristic, like an interest or background, or demographic factors, like gender, race, or disability. Employee resource groups can help new hires feel welcomed, provide mentorship, and increase diversity in the workplace (Goode, in Goode and Dixon 2016). Disability employee resource groups provide an invaluable perspective, often bringing together disabled employees, their allies, and family members of people with disabilities to ensure the workplace represents employees with disabilities and provides support. They also improve the company by bringing in outside speakers, presenters, and training on diversity and inclusion issues relating to the theme of the group (I have been fortunate to consult with several disability employee resource groups on company-wide neurodiversity education). Some industries are more receptive to neurodiversity-specific employee resource groups—Verizon Media and Yahoo!, for instance, have one specifically for neurodiversity, and have created awareness campaigns to help celebrate the strengths of employees with autism, ADHD, OCD (obsessive-compulsive disorder), and other neurodiverse traits and conditions.

Your workplace might have employee resource groups, but there is no existing one for disability or neurodiversity in particular. You might think it is a great idea to start one! To get started, talk to your employer or their human resources department about your idea for an employee resource group. Have a mission statement and goals outlined for your proposed group. A disability group would probably aim to make new people feel included, provide mentorship and support (something we don't get enough of), and help with diversity training. You might want to make some friends at work and recruit your colleagues as members, either through word of mouth, flyers, social media, or some other creative way to get people excited about your cause. Then, once you're all on board, you can start event planning and building a community of like-minded individuals with similar experiences, or who want to be better allies to you and others like you.

STAYING OUT OF TROUBLE

You learned how to be a good community member; you are now a good listener, trying to get involved at work, school, or in other organizations. You are an effective self-advocate. But you also need to stay out of trouble, however possible: be aware of the actions of those around you, follow the law, and cooperate with investigations while also knowing your rights and being aware of the injustices that autistic people face. It's not always easy, but you have the power to do the right thing and to make smart decisions.

Being aware of your surroundings and self

Staying out of trouble doesn't just mean obeying the law and doing your part to do the morally correct thing or somehow avoiding getting fired from a job, for example. Staying out of trouble is also a harm reduction strategy, and being alert, even when we don't want to be too conscious of the world around us.

Unfortunately, part of being an autistic woman in this world for me means sometimes feeling afraid and also hyper-aware of those around me. Sometimes it means I will keep the music in my headphones low. That way, I can hear enough of the world around me to know if there is danger nearby. I'll look over my shoulder one too many times to make sure I am not being followed; I've been followed by a stranger in college when I got off a public bus and went into a grocery store, and the experience made me rightfully nervous. I know if I catch someone's attention in a way that makes me feel afraid. I try not to go out alone at night. I took self-defense classes. To me, all of these things are related to being an autistic female—I am seen as vulnerable because of my gender identity, and I am also at a disadvantage (visible or not) because of my autism.

Some strategies to stay safe do involve a degree of masking, like walking with confidence. Even if you're lost, the illusion of knowing where you are going can detract unwanted attention or dangerous situations with predatory people. Acting like you know where you are going in a big city can be one of the strongest defenses you have.

If you are impaired in some way, from drinking, lack of sleep, medication, or other substances, make sure you always have a plan to get to and from somewhere. You do not want to be alone without a plan. We're taught from the time we're young that talking to strangers is bad, and you never know what can happen.

Interacting with law enforcement and first responders

When you are a young autistic person of any age, chances are neurotypical adults have had conversations with you about police officers and law enforcement. After all, approximately one in five autistic adolescents and young adults will interact with a police officer before the age of 21 (CHOP 2019). The first time I remember my parents talking to me about the police, I was 13 years old. We went to the Autism Society of America's annual conference together that summer because I was invited to speak on a panel (it was my first time speaking publicly about autism). During the downtime, we checked out the different exhibitors, and my mom bought a deck of cards that you could keep in your wallet that explained what autism was and to hand out to family, friends, teachers, or possibly even a police officer. She told me to keep a few in my bag at all times. The cards made a resurgence when I got my learner's permit and was driving; I was told to keep them in my wallet and in my glove box in case I was ever pulled over and the officer gave me permission to hand one to him because it might explain my nervousness, a potential meltdown, or anything else that seemed odd or suspicious. Oh, and I was always told to respect an officer's authority. Looking back, my neurotypical, mostly white, peers at my school probably did not talk about the police growing up, but this is common for children and teens who are disabled, autistic, or people of color.

I've been fortunate not to have had too many police interactions other than when I was with allies and friends, but I recall one time walking home to my apartment with a takeout pizza box through an outdoor mall when a security guard (or was it a police officer?) stopped me, questioning whether I was violating the curfew for teenagers. I wondered if my body language looked suspicious, or if it was just that my face looked younger than one belonging to a 21-year-old woman. Even though I had been taught how to best interact as an autistic person with law enforcement officials, I still felt afraid: I saw the gun in his holster, the way he asked to see my ID and questioned why I was out past curfew. I froze, then calmly explained I was not a teenager (presenting my ID) and was just taking the pizza home. He thanked me, but I was afraid, and spent days wondering why in particular I had been stopped when there were visibly teenagers in the mall area violating the curfew and the guard had not stopped to check their IDs. Was it autism-related or just a stroke of bad luck in a crowded place on a weeknight?

The discussion about autism and the police is so common that police departments across the country are undertaking to train their officers and first responders to better interact with autistic people. When I was a college student, I was approached to help train a Miami area police department on how to interact with autistic people. I narrated a training video alongside a now-retired lieutenant (who has a son on the autism spectrum) from the police department to help bring clarity to interactions between first responders and autistic teens and adults. In the video, police officers learned how to better interact and communicate with autistic adults who may have witnessed a crime or car accident, those who are pulled over while driving, or who might be questioned because of their behavior or affect. The video ultimately taught autistic people how to advocate for themselves by using a special card designating their disability status to help people be more understanding. Times have changed, however, and a card can have negative implications for autistic people who are perceived to be reaching for a weapon, for instance. This is why for people with disabilities, including autism, a medic alert, or disability identification bracelet is a safer alternative to disclosure: the police have experience with bracelets that identify disabilities, and it might be particularly helpful for nonspeaking autistic people to disclose if they do not have access to a communication device.

Why is it that autistic people are more likely to be misunderstood or interacting with police officers compared with other groups of people? There are two camps of interactions: being tangled up in the criminal justice system because you are seen as suspicious-acting (or maybe you did do something wrong), or being a victim or witness to an incident. Bystanders and officers might find autistic people suspicious because we stim, move in atypical ways, or might appear under the influence of drugs or alcohol or be perceived as mentally ill. We might not make eye contact or understand the directions we are being given, or the interaction might trigger a meltdown. These behaviors might be viewed as threatening, and that is how autistic people become needless victims of police brutality and violence—the very people who are supposed to help us in crises are the ones who end up hurting us.

While not every situation where someone acts differently is an emergency or indicative of criminal activity or victimization, well-intended people often believe law enforcement and first responders are necessary—but the consequences for autistic people can be dire.

Police interactions for autistic people of all ages are stressful at best, and could be deadly at worst. Up to half of all people killed by the police are disabled, according to a Ruderman Family Foundation White Paper (McNamara 2017), and people with disabilities are three times more likely to be victims of violent crimes (Harrell 2017). Concerns about unfavorable police interactions and violence are amplified for autistic people of color. Several years ago, my friend Eric Garcia wrote an article for the *Daily Beast* about what it feels like being an autistic person of color interacting with and fearing law enforcement, nicely summing it up as living in "a world that fears my skin color and doesn't want to understand how my brain works" (Garcia 2016).

Together, we must be partners in reducing unnecessary violence and fear against autistic people. As the Autism Society of America wrote in a statement on the unnecessary shooting of Linden Cameron, an unarmed 13-year-old autistic teen in Salt Lake City, Utah, "community services and supports are essential for individuals and families with autism. When a parent, caretaker, or autistic individual relies on first responders to provide crisis intervention, they should not have to worry whether their lives are in danger from the trained professionals sent to help" (Autism Society of America 2020). Due to the nature of this section, it is written with parents, community members, and autistic self-advocates in mind.

- *Establish "community watch" programs to keep autistic people safe.* Reducing emergency calls is a strategy to reduce law enforcement interactions with autistic community members. A 2019 study suggests "community watch" programs created by autistic people and their families can reduce calls and encounters with law enforcement (Soares *et al.* 2019).

  In these community watch initiatives, neighbors and others are in touch with the families and autistic people about autistic behaviors, suspicious or dangerous activity, and safety concerns. As a safety initiative, get to know your neighbors. While knowing your neighbors and acquainting them with you and your autism might seem smart, it is also good for you to know your neighbors in the event of an emergency or something scary. Once, while I was living at home with my family, I heard a bunch of loud booming noises early in the morning. My dad was at work and my mom was running errands, so I was home alone. Something told me the noises must be far away, but they scared me and my pets. I did not know who to call or talk to (I thought it was rude to knock on someone's door so early in the morning, and I did not call the police because I did not believe anyone was hurt), so I waited until my mom came home—she then called the neighbors to ask about the sounds I had heard. The neighbors were all in contact with one another and decided the noises were pranksters setting off fireworks. My mom then proceeded to give me the phone numbers and contact information for the neighbors in case I was ever home alone and needed anything. I instantly felt safer.

Today, your community watch might also be enhanced with neighborhood and community social media groups if you don't know everyone in your neighborhood or apartment building. Depending on your comfort level, apps like NextDoor might be a safer first step than inviting first responders when an autistic person is involved.

- *Autistic adults, their loved ones, friends, and roommates should have a crisis or safety plan.* Many autistic adults have co-occurring mental health disabilities, so having a mental health crisis plan can avoid unnecessary police involvement and the potential for violence. In cases like those of 13-year-old Linden Cameron (his mother called crisis intervention for a mental health episode to help Cameron get to the hospital) and 24-year-old Kayden Clarke (there was a call because Clarke was suicidal), the police were responding to what they believed were dangerous mental health emergencies; both of these autistic people were shot, with Cameron sustaining serious injuries and Clarke being killed. To reduce 911 calls in the event of a mental health crisis, autistic self-advocates and those who live with, support, and know them should develop crisis plans. Have a plan for public and private places. In public, assure people that the situation is under control, so an observer does not call 911.

A crisis plan might be as simple as having a first person to call or respond to the situation. If an autistic person is struggling with their mental health, they should not be alone. Making sure they are in a safe, not sensory overwhelming space to avoid further crisis or a meltdown is a good start, as is reassuring them that you are here for them and care. Communication is key—make sure to phrase things or write them out in a way we can understand and process.

Even in the event of a meltdown or period of autistic burnout (which an unsuspecting neurotypical might interpret as a serious mental health crisis), it is important to care for us or to let us know you are there. When the autistic person feels better, or before a meltdown or burnout happens, have an honest conversation about what a meltdown or burnout looks like for them so it is not mistaken for an event that might lead to law enforcement becoming involved, since most likely, a meltdown or autistic burnout does not make someone harmful to themselves or others.

Police involvement should be a last resort. Before turning to the police in a crisis, you can turn to family members, mental health counseling, hospitalization, a crisis hotline, or disability services. Mental health crises can result in hospitalization or the need for treatment, but no one should be fearing violence or further stress and anxiety from police officers who are not typically equipped to de-escalate situations related to autism and mental health.

- *The police should work with community stakeholders and mental health professionals.* Since a lot of police involvement is a result of crisis management, this builds on the tips of crisis planning. Police officers are not mental health experts or professionals. They are also not experts on autism, as much as we would like them to be, and would like autism awareness training within police departments to be the norm. Not all police departments have received comprehensive autism training, any disability awareness training, or know how to best interact with autistic people. Collaboration between mental health professionals, crisis intervention resources and organizations, law enforcement, disability advocacy organizations, autistic people, and other autism community stakeholders can make interactions more favorable or lead to police departments referring a situation to someone more qualified to handle it. Having psychologists and social workers on staff or who are better equipped to assist autistic people and their families may ease an already fraught situation.

- *Learn how to interact with first responders in a true emergency.* If you, an autistic person, are stopped by a law enforcement or public safety officer, whatever you do, do not attempt to leave the situation without permission. Depending on the situation, it can be seen as resisting arrest or that you are being uncooperative. Try your best to remain calm. The situation is probably scary, but acting or appearing visibly nervous might make things worse—if your hands move too much, it might lead to force being used to restrain or hurt you.

  If you are brought in for police questioning, you have rights. While you might want to say anything to get out of the situation, it is important to know if you are suspected of anything, or if you are questioned, you do not have to immediately answer questions. In some states, you might be able to have a professional or parent present (such as in Florida, due to the Wes Kleinert Fair

Interview Act). Other than stating your name, address, age, and other personal information, you can say you would like a lawyer present.

- *Autistic people should be aware of what looks "suspicious" to neurotypicals.* A lot of focus of autism training on law enforcement expects high levels of autistic masking, so that we avoid appearing suspicious. While I know how masking is a coping mechanism that leads to high levels of burnout, sometimes it is also important to recognize why and how certain behaviors of ours can be interpreted the wrong way. Behavior like pacing back and forth in front of a public place can look like you are looking to rob the place.

Accused or brought in for interrogation

People on the spectrum can still be brought in for police questioning as a suspect or accused person. If you are brought in for police questioning, you have what are called the Miranda rights, which were established through a court cased called *Miranda v. Arizona*. Miranda rights are meant to keep people from incriminating themselves, and are especially important for people with intellectual and developmental disabilities, who may feel coerced into giving a false confession to leave an already distressing situation with law enforcement (Salseda et al. 2011). Autistic people are particularly vulnerable to coercion tactics.

Depending on where you live, law enforcement investigators will read you some version of the Miranda rights if you are in custody and are not free to leave whenever you would like: (1) you have the right to remain silent; (2) anything you say can and will be used against you in a court of law; and (3) you have the right to an attorney—if you can't afford one, one will be appointed. If you waive these rights, the questioning will continue. If you invoke them and speak up, be clear and concise, and then the questioning will end. Silence is not the same as admitting guilt. Clearly voice that you would like to speak to an attorney—do not leave room for interpretation ("I want an attorney" has no room for error, while "I *think* I want an attorney" does).

ELECTIONS AND VOTING IN THE US: YOUR VOICE, YOUR CHOICE

It was August 2012, and I was right outside the dining hall at the University of Florida campus when a student approached me about registering to vote for the very first time. I knew voting was important. I did not pre-register when I was 17, nor did I register when I turned 18 a month earlier. I enthusiastically signed up, knowing a presidential election was coming in November, though admittedly I was not as informed as I would have liked to have been about what was happening in my college town to be able to vote for anyone other than the president. The student who approached me helped me fill out the application. On Election Day, I stood in line for well over an hour at the student union building to cast my very first ballot and vote for my choice for the president of the United States, as well as who else might be representing me statewide and locally in my college town. I cried tears of happiness that afternoon, calling my parents to tell them I had voted in my very first election. I would go on to make a point of voting in every other race possible. Since then, I have now voted in three presidential elections (2012, 2016, and 2020) and felt that same pride as when I stood in line surrounded by students in 2012.

One of the greatest rights you have as an adult and US citizen is the right to vote. Voting is a way to use your voice in the decision to choose our elected officials, pass laws or amendments, and make other decisions within state and federal government. At the federal level, we can vote for the president and members of Congress (members of the US House of Representatives and members of the US Senate). At the state and local level, we can vote for candidates vying to run for governor or positions in the state senate, assembly, or house, or we can vote for people representing us at the county level as sheriffs, judges, and commissioners, and for our towns and cities as mayors and commissioners. All of these politicians and people have the power to make decisions that impact each of our lives, and they are hired to do their jobs by people like you and me.

Registering to vote

You need to register to vote! Sometimes it isn't as simple as it was for me, where a random student with a voter registration drive walks up to you and asks if you're registered, you say no, and they help you fill out the application and mail it for you.

To register, you need to be at least 18 years old. Depending on where you live, registering to vote means you need to fill out a form online, or in person (at your local Motor Vehicles Administration or Department of Motor Vehicles, city hall, or state or local election office), or you can print and mail the registration to the designated elections officials where you live. If you have never registered to vote or have moved, check your state's Secretary of State website or your country's comparable to see when the deadlines to vote before the next elections are. In some states, you need a government-issued photo ID and to provide the numbers on it to say you are who you claim to be on your registration—these IDs are either a state-issued ID card or your driver's license.

On your registration, you also pick a political party. If you don't feel comfortable picking a major political party, you can pick "independent" or no party affiliation. Depending on your state, deciding on no party affiliation might mean you are not allowed to vote in a partisan primary election (in Florida, you must be registered as either a Republican or Democrat to vote in either of the two primaries). Primaries are elections that narrow the field of candidates running for office down to one candidate per party—if you feel you have a favorite you agree with, and want them to advance to a general election, you might want to register with a party affiliation if your state has closed party primaries.

How elections work

In the US, once you are registered to vote, you will be able to vote in primary elections, general elections, and special elections.

You are allowed to request an absentee ballot, which lets you get a ballot in the mail to an address of your choosing that you fill out and then send back or drop off at the local elections office. One of the biggest advantages of absentee ballots is that you can fill them out from the comfort of your own home, which means you can avoid early voting or Election Day crowds and lines, or an inaccessible polling place. They also give you a bit more time to research the lesser known candidates or issues.

You can also vote during the early voting period in person, if your state has one. Make sure you bring your state ID or driver's license if photo ID is required in order to vote. For early voting, check which polling places you are allowed to vote at. I voted early in person in two elections at my local library, and it was very quiet and quick. I felt confident and received the "I Voted!" sticker, which made me feel really cool when I arrived at work (voting at the library began early in the morning, so I went before work). If you don't vote with an absentee or mail ballot or early voting, your only other option is to vote in person on Election Day at the polling place that your voter registration says you must vote at. If it is a primary or special election, your state determines what date the election is held; for federal general elections, Election Day is the first Tuesday in November.

On your ballot, fill in the ovals next to the candidate or law you choose. Sign where your signature is requested and submit the ballot in the mail or into the voting machines as directed. If you vote in person, you'll get a sticker saying you voted.

After voting, election results are calculated once the polls are closed. Most people get the election results on TV or through the internet. The newly elected officials take their oaths of office once the election results are certified, and constitutional amendments or new ballot initiatives go into effect depending on when the law says they will. In certain states, if a candidate did not win the majority (50.1 percent or more) of the vote, they will advance to a runoff race, which is a separate election you will vote in.

As people with disabilities, we have certain rights while voting. If you need help while voting, you are allowed to bring someone with you as a support. Poll workers, or folks who work to help make elections run smoothly, are also able to help you read voting forms and use the voting machines that scan your ballot. You are entitled to a safe, accessible polling place, and to vote independently and securely.

How to be informed on social and political issues

A lot of candidates want your attention during primaries and in the months leading up to the election. You might get flyers in the mail, campaign workers knocking on your door, or unwanted phone calls, text messages, or emails from campaign staffers and candidates. But how do you sort through the noise of what is important and who you agree with, and how do you get information on the local races that might not be as well known as the presidential election?

You can receive information about the candidates and their ideas and platforms through news media, such as on TV, the internet, social media, or newspapers. To inform voters, candidates often participate in debates and town halls where they share their ideas and try to convince voters why they are better for the job than their opponents. At a town hall, you might be able to ask the candidate a question or hear other people's questions about how they would do the job, or how they feel about specific issues.

For local elections and ballot initiatives (such as taxes, state constitutional amendments, or new laws), the best place to learn about those issues is often your local news. For instance, a lot of people do not know much about the races for judicial candidates because judges are nonpartisan and do not host debates. Even as a lawyer, I did not appear in every judge's courtroom, so it was difficult to know how they acted or what their records were. To stay informed about those types of races, I would read the local newspapers or legal news. Newspaper editorial boards also put out a slate of endorsements, trying to encourage voters to pick certain candidates and to vote a certain way on initiatives because they feel those are the best qualified people after meeting with candidates, and have carefully analysed the language of the proposed initiatives as well. Sometimes the language of ballot initiatives can be sneaky, so the newspaper endorsements and coverage can be extremely valuable to know why something may be helpful or harmful to your local community.

If you are interested in disability issues and where political candidates and legislators stand on disability-related policies, you can follow #CripTheVote. This is a nonpartisan online movement activating and engaging disabled people on policies and practices important to the disability community. Through Twitter chats, #CripTheVote has hosted conversations about the accessibility of polling places, question and answer sessions, and chats with presidential candidates, and given information on disability policy platforms.

Following social issues can happen outside of elections, too, so make sure to continue to stay informed so you can see what your elected officials are doing, to either vote for someone different next time or help hold them accountable.

THE US CENSUS

A required part of our political process is the US Census. Every decade, the federal government attempts to count how many people live within the US and inside each household. You (or the head of your household) will get a card in the mail with instructions of how to be counted in the Census. When answering questions from a census worker over the phone, by mail, or through the online form, the head of the household will count every person living in the house as well as their sex, age, and race. Filling out the Census is important because it determines how many representatives each state will have in Congress for the next 10 years, provide data that helps communities, and determines how much money your community might receive in assistance from federal government. If you have an executive functioning failure and forget to fill out the Census, a census worker will follow up at your address, in person.

JURY DUTY IN THE US

Along with being able to vote, one of the other acts of service you get the privilege of when you turn 18 is serving on a jury. Juries are groups of community members who are sworn in by the court to weigh evidence in a case and give a verdict. You can have juries of either 6 or 12 people making decisions in civil cases (determining liability, and if someone has to pay money) or criminal cases (determining if someone is guilty, and jail or prison sentencing).

If you are summoned for jury duty, you will receive a notice in the mail telling you what day and courthouse to show up at. Unless you have a valid reason to fill out an excuse or exemption form, you are required to report for jury duty. You can get arrested for not reporting at the proper place at the time you are summoned.

For autistic people, jury duty can be difficult because it is a huge disruptor in routine—although it is a reason you are allowed to miss work, and your employer can't hold it against you. If you are selected for a jury at trial, it might be uncertain whether or not the trial will be for a few hours, days, or weeks. Other routine disruptions associated with jury service are harder to anticipate, like the size of the crowds waiting to be called for jury duty, lighting and noise, or how long you will be waiting before the start of a trial.

To make jury service easier, some might bring a letter or other tool to explain to lawyers once they are called for jury selection what accommodations they may need if they are selected to serve on the jury. If you need formal accommodations for jury duty or jury service, each judicial circuit has an Americans with Disabilities Act (ADA) coordinator who works on disability accommodations for lawyers, jurors, witnesses, and others who participate in the legal system.

OBEYING THE LAW

One of the most important things you will do as a member of a community is to follow the law to stay out of trouble. This means, of course, doing your part in not doing anything criminal or illegal and using good judgment. We interact with the law far more often than we think: whether it is when we cross the street, are driving (or will be driving), or choosing not to use illegal substances. Obeying the law is like following the rules of the game; if you don't follow the rules, you might owe fines, or worse, end up interacting with the criminal justice system. And sometimes we don't always know the hard and fast rules or what to do if we end up breaking them.

DRIVING AND RULES OF THE ROAD

Learning to drive

I was the last one of my friends to get my driver's license because I was simply a nervous driver, and often, figuring out the spatial awareness of parking has proven to be a struggle. While I am not a frequent driver, it is a skill I have and feel more independent for knowing. It is okay if you don't drive and choose to rely on friends, family, caregivers, rideshares or other methods of transportation to get places, but for the young adult or autistic adult who wants to learn to drive, a few things made the process infinitely less stressful for my neurodivergent self:

- *Choose a car you feel comfortable driving.* You can rent a car temporarily, borrow another person's car to learn in, or buy or lease your own car. Every car has a different learning curve and different instructions to go along with it. I recommend starting with an automatic transmission to ease the learning curve a little (I still don't know how to drive a manual transmission/stick shift). Some factors that might help you determine if it's the right car for you are your needs for space, blind spots and visibility, reliability, price, or gas mileage.

- *Learn somewhere "easy."* Learning in a crowded place or on busy highways can be extremely scary and stressful. When I was learning to drive, my dad and I would take the car on a Sunday morning to a large, corporate parking lot. Nobody would be there except for the security guard, who was okay with me learning how to drive around and park, reverse, and use the brakes and gas. It was a lot less stressful, and when I felt more experienced, we gradually began driving on less crowded streets, parking in places with other cars around, and when I felt ready, I took the highway.

- If you want to learn with someone who might be more understanding of autism or caters to different learning styles, *sign up for a driver's education program or take private lessons*. I also took supplemental lessons because there were things that my dad did not feel comfortable teaching me right away, like driving on the highway. Cars used in driver's education and lessons might also have brakes on the passenger side for safety and to help you learn (though I always found this jarring). My teacher was understanding and helped eliminate distractions. Lessons or driver's education can also help you qualify for insurance discounts.

- *Build confidence.* As a defensive, nervous driver, I always felt confident with someone else in the car or doing shorter trips compared with longer ones. Another person can always help you continue to learn and find ways to adapt so autism does not become a hindrance to driving (if you choose to drive, of course).

The rules of the road

I was really excited to get my learner's permit when I was 15 years old and wanting to drive for the first time. The process of getting my learner's permit was the first time I would have any familiarity with the many different traffic laws beyond stop signs and traffic lights. The prerequisites to showing up and getting the piece of plastic that would allow me to drive with adult supervision would be the beginning of a real-life driver's education. I had to take an online class about the dangers of drugs and alcohol (both substances can lead to stops, arrests, and charges for driving under the influence) because of concerns about drunk driving and additional impairments. I also had to take a road rules and signs test that measured understanding of the various road signs and when to yield or keep distance between other cars.

Basic educational requirements to have permission to drive from the government do not cover all the grounds you need to know. Even if you have a driver's license (or have it on your bucket list), there are still tons of other rules and procedures that simply aren't taught in driving school or in driving or permit tests. In fact, one of the easiest places to get caught up and interacting with the law, law enforcement, or lawyers is driving. There are all sorts of challenges involved with driving.

Following the law also includes *minimizing distractions*. Driving requires focus, so it's best to avoid anything that could impair your judgment and could cause harm to yourself or others due to inattention. Do not text while you are driving—you can cause an accident or be stopped by law enforcement for texting behind the wheel. If you have to talk on the phone, be sure to use Bluetooth or other hands-free technology so your hands remain on the wheel.

If you do have an accident, do not say it is your fault. First, make sure everyone is okay. Call 911 if anyone is hurt or appears hurt. Then file an accident report with the police, where you and the other driver/car owner/passengers/witnesses will recount what happened. Then call your insurance company in case of any damage or to put them on alert.

If you're driving, you should *have your driver's license or learner's permit with you*. It is probably going to be in your wallet, so take your wallet. Earlier in this book we talked about taking your driver's license with you as a form of government-issued photo ID for most things, and when you're driving, it's proof that you are a licensed driver, which an officer will ask for if you get pulled over. In addition, you should also have your *registration*. Do not, however, pull out these documents unless an officer asks for them.

WHAT HAPPENS IF YOU NEED A LAWYER

I'd like to clear this up with you—you do not only need a lawyer if you get into trouble and are arrested and have charges pending against you. You can be in need of a lawyer for criminal or civil legal proceedings. Criminal proceedings are exactly that: you are likely accused of a crime and a defense attorney or public defender (who is appointed to represent you if you cannot afford a lawyer) is there to make sure you eventually have your day in court, since you have the right to trial and your day in court.

In civil proceedings, you might have been discriminated against, in a car accident, be escaping domestic violence, in a dispute with your landlord—basically, anything that involves protecting and upholding your rights or an entitlement to money.

Civil lawyers or litigators are easy to find. If you don't know where to start, call your state bar association, which has lawyer referral programs. If you can't afford a lawyer, check out your local legal aid organization, which in the US you can locate through LawHelp.org. Legal aid may be able to provide free or low-cost legal representation based on your level of income. For private lawyers, you can also use the lawyer referral services, the internet, remember whose faces and names you saw on advertisements, or see who comes recommended for certain areas of law.

If you need a lawyer in a criminal proceeding where you are accused of a crime, you can be appointed a public defender if you do not have the money to afford a private lawyer. You might want to tell your lawyer you are autistic and how autism affects you, since it might be part of their strategy to persuade the prosecutors (lawyers for the government) to lessen or dismiss charges.

No matter what, when you get a lawyer (I spend a lot of time teaching lawyers how to interact with neurodivergent clients, witnesses, and others within the legal system), communication is key. It's okay to bring stim toys with you or to meet somewhere else—lawyers should be accommodating to you. However, they might be mindful or concerned that bringing a support person means that what you say to the lawyer might not be confidential under the attorney–client privilege. Emotional support people destroy that privilege, while an interpreter does not (if you are nonspeaking, your lawyer might try to say this person is an interpreter so what you say is secret in those meetings and the other side can't use what you say).

Working with lawyers as a client and preparing for hearings, proceedings, or what to do can be exhausting, but knowing where to start and having the right team of accommodating and understanding counsel can make the experience better and lead to a more favorable outcome for you.

KNOWING YOUR RIGHTS AND LAWS THAT INTERACT WITH YOU, EXPLAINED BY A LAWYER

As autistic people, we regularly interact with the world around us. We always talk about following the law and obeying the rules, but sometimes, other people do not obey the rules or enforce them. As autistic people, we are part of the greater disabled community. As people with disabilities, we are entitled to certain rights to access and accommodations to be independent. If other people do not grant you reasonable accommodations, or treat you differently on the basis of disability or autism, you might be able to take action by hiring a lawyer, beginning an investigation, or filing a civil lawsuit (which means someone or somewhere might have to fix the issue, and may also owe money for their wrongdoing).

A lot of us are not lawyers, and frankly, if I hadn't gone to law school and have exposure to the different areas of law that interact with us as autistic people on a daily basis, I might not have known about the extent of protections that disabled people are entitled to. Reading court decisions applying the law or understanding the language Congress passed into legislation can be confusing—often, legal writing and government statutes are not written in plain language or a way that most adults can easily understand. To help you understand your rights, I'm going to break down some of the major laws that autistic people interact with in an accessible way. There are only a few major pieces of disability rights-only laws: the Americans with Disabilities Act (ADA), the Rehabilitation Act, and the Individuals with Disabilities Education Act (IDEA).

However, these explanations do not constitute legal advice—I am only licensed to practice law in the state of Florida, and cannot provide legal advice or represent clients outside of the state of Florida. I also do not currently practice in disability law, so my experience and knowledge is as a result of research, lived experience, and exposure to disability law topics. If you need a lawyer because of a disability-related issue, check out your local nonprofit legal aid societies or your state's member organization of the National Disability Rights Network, and they may be able to either take your case or point you in the right direction of a lawyer who can help.

The Americans with Disabilities Act (ADA)

The Americans with Disabilities Act (ADA) is a federal law in the US that does not allow people with disabilities to be discriminated against or treated differently because they have a disability. It was signed into law in 1990 by Former President George H.W. Bush and amended to protect more people in 2008 by Former President Barack Obama. The ADA does not allow unequal treatment in wanting or having a job, state and local government programs, services or buildings, public places like parks and businesses, telecommunications, and other programs. The ADA allows people with disabilities to be part of their communities!

The ADA is divided into five titles, or sections. Title I discusses employment, Title II handles issues of discrimination, accommodation, and access in state and local government entities, Title III is about public accommodations and places, Title IV governs telecommunications, and Title V is a catch-all for things that aren't covered by the other four titles. For autistic people, most of the issues we face are covered under Titles I, II, and/or III.

Under Title I, employers with more than 15 employees are not allowed to discriminate against people with disabilities at any stage of the employment process, which means they cannot knowingly treat people with disabilities negatively on job applications, at interviews, or on the job, pay them less because of a disability, or fire them because of a disability. Title I also entitles autistic employees to *reasonable accommodations* to help them perform their job responsibilities, as long as these do not cause an undue burden on the employer, such as being impossible, incredibly difficult, or extremely expensive. We talked a bit about job accommodations earlier, but if your employer denies accommodations, you might be able to file a charge alleging discrimination on the basis of autism and disability with the US Equal Opportunity Employment Commission.

Titles II and III are more expansive and include community settings, public places, and state and local government entities. They must also be accessible to people with disabilities and be able to provide reasonable accommodations. Buildings must be built to certain standards for disability access. You should not be excluded from community settings, buildings, or activities on the basis of disability.

KEY TAKEAWAYS

- The ADA protects autistic and disabled people from discrimination.

- You are able to receive reasonable accommodations at work, school, or other community settings.

The Rehabilitation Act

The Rehabilitation Act of 1973 is an extensive piece of legislation that was the precursor to the ADA and affects entities and agencies that receive money from the US federal government. In your life, that might be colleges and universities as well as specific employers. Under Section 503, federal contractors or subcontractors are required to take affirmative action to recruit, hire, promote, and retain employees with disabilities. Section 504 prohibits discrimination against individuals with disabilities in any program or activity receiving federal financial assistance. If you have an autism diagnosis, you are able to seek protection and accommodations in all federally funded programs—employment, housing, community living, and education—under this law.

The Individuals with Disabilities Education Act (IDEA)

While you may be an adult, this might not be the most important law in your toolbox. The Individuals with Disabilities

Education Act (IDEA) gives students with disabilities access to special education services and a "free and appropriate" public education until they graduate high school or reach the age of 22, whichever comes first. Under the IDEA you might have received an IEP detailing the goals of your academic studies or accommodations. If you went to public school or are still in public school, you might still be able to use services you received under the IDEA to help you receive accommodations in higher education under the Rehabilitation Act. Some of this can be used as proof of disability in other settings, depending on the context.

Medicaid Home and Community-Based Services

In the US, autistic adults who have additional support needs might be able to get help through Medicaid waivers for home and community-based services. To see if you are eligible for these services, contact your local or state developmental disability agency. State and local developmental disability services are funded through these Medicaid Home and Community-Based Services (HCBS) waivers. HCBS can help provide healthcare and long-term services and support within the home or community for adults on the autism spectrum. Some of these services include case management, day health services, day and residential habilitation, and home health aides. HCBS programs may also have a long waiting list. For more information on Medicaid Home and Community-Based Services, visit Medicaid.gov.

Social Security

In the US, one of the major programs that helps adults with disabilities, autism included, is Social Security benefits. People with qualifying disabilities—including autism—might be eligible for assistance under the programs administered by the Social Security Administration if they have a medical diagnosis. The two major programs assisting people with disabilities are Social Security Disability Insurance (SSDI) and Social Security Income (SSI). SSDI pays benefits to you and possibly family members if you paid Social Security taxes and worked for a long enough period of time (this changes each year). There are screening tools to see if you are eligible for SSDI. SSI pays benefits to those with disabilities or who are over the age of 65 who have limited income and resources so they can afford basic living needs and expenses. If you are unable to find employment, you might be reliant on Social Security for income. Social Security might offer you incentives to allow you to work while maintaining your benefits, such as the Plan for Achieving Self Support (PASS), the Impairment Related Work Expenses (IRWE) program, and the Ticket to Work program.

Note that access to Social Security programs is also a disability rights issue, as many disabled activists criticize how they have had to either avoid marriage or get divorced in order to protect their income from Social Security, sharing that true equality has not yet been achieved for disabled people if we are forced to choose between income and access to services, or love.

DREAMING BIG IN CIVIC ENGAGEMENT

You did it! You are a master of self-advocacy; you got involved in your community. It really is a big world out there, and outside of goodwill, volunteering, and social justice education is a potential exciting next step. You took the first step towards civic engagement by becoming a voter (maybe you voted too), and now you want to see how the people you voted for are doing their job—or you want to put pressure on them, or possibly be an elected official yourself.

Holding elected officials accountable

People hire elected officials by voting for them, and the main way they get fired is when they are voted out—it is not as often they resign or are forced out of office. As a constituent, you have the ability to influence how your lawmakers vote in meetings and legislative sessions locally, statewide, or at federal level. You can call offices to voice your support or opposition to a certain issue.

The most powerful tool there is to voice your concerns is at a town hall, where the elected official has an official gathering or meeting with their constituents to update them on what's going on in government or their job and takes questions. Town halls are a powerful opportunity to ask questions that you think matter—and demand answers on the spot rather than be at the mercy of hoping your email or phone calls are received and corresponded with.

Of course, if you're disappointed with who represents you, you can sign up to advocate for specific issues through other groups and community organizing. You can advocate for policy as a lobbyist or community member, or join coalitions. You can volunteer on a political campaign for that person's opponent. Or, of course, you can always challenge them yourself.

Policy change and lobbying

I never thought I would care about policy change or lobbying before. I never took a government or civics class in high school, and I did not major in political science or intern for a lobbying firm or politician's office. Yet, as part of my nonprofit board service, I was asked to accompany the organization's executive director and others on an annual lobbying trip to Florida's capital city in order to advocate for a state funding increase. While there, I was able to talk to lawmakers about autism along with the needs of autistic people and their families in my community. I found each conversation to be fascinating, and the members of the state house and senate seemed interested in learning more about me and what we had to say. I felt empowered. It was my first lobbying trip, and I hope to someday go to Washington, DC, in order to advocate for something too.

I'm hardly the first autistic or neurodivergent person to go spend time advocating or in policy. ASAN, Autism Speaks, the Autism Society of America, and the Arc of the United States all work on national policy agendas related to autism and intellectual or developmental disabilities. One of my closest autistic friends is a federal relations specialist advocating on behalf of a university system and maintaining relationships with members of Congress in DC.

To figure out what policy you might be interested in advocating for, think about causes and concerns that mean a lot to you, that lawmakers at the local, state, and federal level may overlook or not give enough attention to. My local women lawyers' association lobbies for courthouses to have places for mothers to breastfeed their babies, while our state-funded autism resource centers advocate for more funding to serve more people. Others champion different causes, like gun violence, access to healthcare for people with disabilities, funding for programs, or other things related to safety or an organization's interests.

The Arc annually holds a Disability Policy Summit for self-advocates and stakeholders with intellectual and developmental disabilities, which could be an invaluable learning experience. Similarly, most state developmental disability councils host a program called Partners in Policymaking, which should be free or low cost to attend, and teaches disability community stakeholders and self-advocates about disability history and how to be more effective political advocates.

One of the ongoing policy efforts I am involved with in some way statewide is about supported decision-making. Disability Rights Florida began building a broad coalition of self-advocates, disability service providers, families, and eldercare lawyers to come together to help Florida law include alternatives to guardianship. The effort includes meeting as a team, a lawyer who wrote the language of the bill and asked us to critique it, figure out who we can get as organizational sponsors to build the coalition, and to decide which lawmakers might be potential sponsors or champions for our cause. It has been an enlightening experience, and shows that being involved in the process can be as much or as little as you'd like—I have given suggestions for new coalition members and read the language of the bill, but I do not often have the time to make the monthly meetings. Depending on how things go further in the process, maybe I will get to go back to the state capital and help lobby lawmakers and tell them why supported decision-making is important for autistic and disabled adults.

Running for office and other political opportunities

When everyone was focused on the big wins and surprises of Election Night 2020, the historic wins are the ones that resonated most with me. One of those wins belonged to Jessica Benham, a Democrat in Pennsylvania, who made history as the first openly autistic candidate to win a seat in the state legislature. Benham is not the first autistic statewide politician (Briscoe Cain, a Republican in Texas, and Yuh-Line Niou, a Democrat in New York, are both autistic state legislators), but the first who made it central to her campaign and was elected to represent her district in the state house.

Elected officials like Benham, Cain, and Niou should not be a small minority. We have yet to have an autistic member of Congress so far, though we have had parents of children with disabilities and other folks with disabilities serve in the House and Senate.

The National Council for Independent Living tracks candidates with disabilities running up and down the ballot, from Congress to local elections. There are far too few recorded candidates with disabilities, let alone with autism. If running for an elected position in your community is something that interests you, check out nonpartisan efforts from reputable organizations like the National Council for Independent Living as well as training on campaigning and filing for candidacy—especially if you are multiply marginalized—from organizations such as She Should Run.

State and local government service

Serving in state and local government can be a valuable way to learn and help others where you live, too, without running for office. Chances are, there is some kind of organization you might want to volunteer or get involved with.

Even if you do not run for office, there are autism- and disability-related positions within the government you can have either as full-time jobs or as appointed board members. Each state has a developmental disabilities council, and a certain number of those seats must belong to self-advocates. State developmental disability councils are federally funded, self-governing organizations that promote self-determination and inclusion, and identify important policy and community needs of people with developmental disabilities. Members of the public can apply and interview for seats on state developmental disability councils and be appointed by the state's governor. The federal government also has opportunities for appointments relating to autism, such as the Interagency Autism Coordinating Committee and the National Council on Disability, which oversee and make recommendations on research and policy that affect autistic and disabled people.

At the local level, you can also get involved in citywide or local efforts. Disability is an "everyone" issue (at some point in our lives, everybody will be disabled), and some places are doing autism-friendly initiatives or are working to be more inclusive of their residents. I was recommended by a few disability community colleagues earlier in 2021 to join my city's disability affairs advisory board and was appointed by a city commissioner. Each month, the disability affairs board meets to discuss issues concerning residents with disabilities; our board is led by a wonderful woman with multiple sclerosis and involves all stakeholders: disabled people, autistic people, and parents of children with disabilities. We talk about the accessibility of community facilities, events, and how we can best support disabled residents. The city issues proclamations in honor of Autism Awareness Month and Disability Employment Awareness Month, and celebrated the anniversary of the ADA this year, and I am pretty sure the disability affairs board had a lot to do with those celebrations and acknowledgments of the disability community. It is one of the coolest volunteer opportunities that exists, and the city commission and local government listen to what we have to say.

Sending You Out into the World

Independence, in actuality, does not exist. Hopefully from reading this book, something resonated with you and either empowered you to try something new or to learn a new skill—or muster up the courage to seek help with something. All we can do is have the strength and vulnerability to acknowledge when we need help. As autistic people, we are valued, loved, and integral parts of society. Our worth is not in how much we do in a job, where we live, who we love, or how much money we make. Our worth is inherent. We deserve to be here and have meaningful, productive lives on our own terms and to speak up for ourselves. That is what true independence is. Independence, as far as I am concerned, is the freedom to be your full, wonderful, autistic self—and the world will just have to accept that. The world better respect you and see how much you deserve to be here, make your mark, take up space, and responsibly do the things you are passionate about!

References

Attwood, Tony (2007) *The Complete Guide to Asperger's Syndrome*. London and Philadelphia, PA: Jessica Kingsley Publishers.

Austin, Robert D. and Gary Pisano (2017) 'Neurodiversity as a competitive advantage.' *Harvard Business Review*, May–June. Available at: https://hbr.org/2017/05/neurodiversity-as-a-competitive-advantage

Autism Society of America (2020) 'The Autism Society calls for better training for law enforcement after the shooting of 13-year-old autistic youth.' September 9. Available at: www.autism-society.org/news/the-autism-society-calls-for-better-training-for-law-enforcement-after-the-shooting-of-13-year-old-autistic-youth/

BBC News (2013) 'Explaining low stamina levels—with spoons.' June 21. Available at: www.bbc.com/news/blogs-ouch-22972767

Butwicka, Agnieszka, Niklas Långström, Henrik Larsson, Sebastian Lundström, *et al.* (2017) 'Increased risk for substance use-related problems in autism spectrum disorders: A population-based cohort study.' *Journal of Autism and Developmental Disorders 47*, 80–9.

CDC (Centers for Disease Control and Prevention) (no date) 'Benefits of physical activity.' Available at: www.cdc.gov/physicalactivity/basics/pa-health/index.htm

Cheak-Zamora, Nancy, Michelle Teti, Clark Peters, and Anna Maurer-Batjer (2017) 'Financial capabilities among youth with autism spectrum disorder.' *Journal of Child and Family Studies 26*, 1310–17. Available at: http://link.springer.com/article/10.1007/s10826-017-0669-9

CHOP (Children's Hospital of Philadelphia) (2019) 'CHOP researchers present new findings at 2019 International Society for Autism Research Annual Meeting.' May 1. Available at: www.chop.edu/news/chop-researchers-present-new-findings-2019-international-society-autism-research-annual-meeting

Coffey, Sarah (2020) 'Checklist: Basic cleaning supplies for a small space.' *Apartment Therapy*, April 15. Available at: www.apartmenttherapy.com/basic-cleaning-supplies-for-a-114200

Dartmouth College (no date) 'Introduction to power, privilege, and social justice.' Office of Pluralism and Leadership. Available at: https://students.dartmouth.edu/opal/education/introduction-power-privilege-and-social-justice

Debt.org (2021) 'Key figures behind America's consumer debt.' January 28. Available at: www.debt.org/faqs/americans-in-debt

Emamzadeh, Arash (2020) 'How to find the right therapist.' *Psychology Today*, January 4. Available at: www.psychologytoday.com/us/blog/finding-new-home/202001/how-find-the-right-therapist

Furfaro, Hannah (2020) 'Sleep problems with autism, explained.' *Spectrum*, February 6. Available at: www.spectrumnews.org/news/sleep-problems-autism-explained

Garcia, Eric (2016) 'What it feels like to be an autistic person of color in the eyes of the police.' *Daily Beast*, July 25. Available at: www.thedailybeast.com/what-it-feels-like-to-be-an-autistic-person-of-color-in-the-eyes-of-the-police

Gholipour, Bahar (2017) 'Short sleep is unhappy bedfellow for autism features.' *Spectrum*, May 8. Available at: www.spectrumnews.org/news/short-sleep-unhappy-bedfellow-autism-features

Goode, Shelton and Isaac Dixon (2016) 'Are employee resource groups good for business?' SHRM, August 25. Available at: www.shrm.org/hr-today/news/hr-magazine/0916/pages/are-employee-resource-groups-good-for-business.aspx

Gratton, Finn V. (no date) 'Finding a therapist who is a food fit for you or your child.' Available at: www.grattonpsychotherapy.com/finding-a-therapist

Harrell, Erika (2017) Crimes Against Persons with Disabilities: 2009–2015 Statistical Tables. US Department of Justice Bureau of Justice Statistics, NCJ No. 250632.

Hensel, Wendy F. (2017) 'People with autism spectrum disorder in the workplace: An expanding legal frontier.' *Harvard Civil Rights – Civil Liberties Law Review 52*. Available at: https://papers.ssrn.com/sol3/papers.cfm?abstract_id=2916911

Hudson, Chloe C., Layla Hall, and Kate L. Harkness (2019) 'Prevalence of depressive disorders in individuals with autism spectrum disorder: A meta-analysis.' *Journal of Abnormal Child Psychology 47*, 1, 165–75.

Hull, Laura, K. V. Petrides, Carrie Allison, Paula Smith, *et al.* (2017) '"Putting on my best normal": Social camouflaging in adults with autism spectrum conditions.' *Journal of Autism and Developmental Disorders 47*, 2519–34.

JAN (Job Accommodation Network) (no date) 'Autism spectrum.' Available at: https://askjan.org/disabilities/Autism-Spectrum.cfm

Kapp, Steven K., Robyn Steward, Laura Crane, et al. (2019) '"People should be allowed to do what they like": Autistic adults' views and experiences of stimming.' Autism 23, 7. Available at: https://doi.org/10.1177/1362361319829628

Lai, Meng-Chuan, Michael V. Lombardo, Amber Nv Ruigrok, Bhismadev Chakrabarti, et al. (2017) 'Quantifying and exploring camouflaging in men and women with autism.' Autism 21, 6, 690–702.

Lindzon, Jared (2019) 'Why companies who hire people with disabilities outperformed their peers.' Fast Company, March 13. Available at: www.fastcompany.com/90311742/why-companies-who-hire-people-with-disabilities-outperformed-their-peers

Luterman, Sara (2020) 'Why businesses can still get away with paying pennies to employees with disabilities.' Vox, March 16. Available at: www.vox.com/identities/2020/3/16/21178197/people-with-disabilities-minimum-wage

McNamara, Brittney (2017) 'Up to half of all people killed by police are disabled.' Teen Vogue, September 29. Available at: www.teenvogue.com/story/half-of-people-killed-by-police-have-disabilities

Mingus, Mia (2017) 'Access intimacy, interdependence, and disability justice.' April 11. Available at: www.youtube.com/watch?v= ONpqOH GlbZM&feature=emb_title

Moss, Haley (2019) 'For autistic people, "benevolent ableism" can be a form of bullying.' Teen Vogue, August 9. Available at: www.teenvogue.com/story/for-autistic-people-benevolent-ableism-can-be-a-form-of-bullying

Moss, Haley (2020) 'How I disclose my disability during a job search.' Fast Company, February 24. Available at: www.fastcompany.com/90466861/how-i-disclose-my-disability-during-a-job-search

Nagele-Piazza, Lisa (2018) 'Workplace bullying and harassment: What's the difference?' SHRM, March 28. Available at: www.shrm.org/resourcesandtools/legal-and-compliance/state-and-local-updates/pages/workplace-bullying.aspx

National Consumer Law Center (2020) Surviving Debt: Expert Advice for Getting Out of Financial Trouble. Available at: https://library.nclc.org/sd/0102

Nimmo-Smith, Victoria, Hein Heuvelman, Christina Dalman, Michael Lundberg, et al. (2020) 'Anxiety disorders in adults with autism spectrum disorder: A population-based study.' Journal of Autism and Developmental Disorders 50, 1, 308–18. Available at: https://pubmed.ncbi.nlm.nih.gov/31621020

OAR (Organization for Autism Research) (no date) 'Self-advocate resources.' Available at: https://researchautism.org/how-we-help/self-advocates/resources-self-advocates

Optum, Inc. (2018) 'The importance of work for individuals with intellectual/ developmental disabilities.' NACBHDD (National Association of County Behavioral Health & Developmental Disability Directors). Available at: www.autism-society.org/wp-content/uploads/2018/04/IDD-BRIEFING-Employment-importance-Final-2.22.18.pdf

Orsmond, Gael I., Paul T. Shattuck, Benjamin P. Cooper, Paul R. Sterzing, and Kristy A. Anderson (2013) 'Social participation among young adults with an autism spectrum disorder.' *Journal of Autism and Developmental Disorders 43*, 2710–19.

Pacific Alliance on Disability Self-Advocacy (2016) 'Conflicting access needs.' Available at: https://pacific-alliance.org/wp-content/uploads/2016/10/PADSA-Resource-Guide-_Conflicting-Access-Needs.pdf

Raymaker, Dora M., Alan R. Teo, Nicole A. Steckler, Brandy Lentz, *et al.* (2020) '"Having all of your internal resources exhausted beyond measure and being left with no clean-up crew": Defining autistic burnout.' *Autism in Adulthood 2*, 2, 132–43. Available at: http://doi.org/10.1089/aut.2019.0079

REACH (Rehabilitation, Education and Advocacy for Citizens with Handicaps, Inc.) (no date) 'What is Independent Living?' Available at: www.reachcils.org/what-independent-living

Rosenfeld, Michael J., Reuben J. Thomas, and Sonia Hausen (2019) 'Disintermediating your friends: How online dating in the United States displaces other ways of meeting.' *PNAS: Proceedings of the National Academy of Sciences 116*, 36, 17753–8. Available at: www.ncbi.nlm.nih.gov/pmc/articles/PMC6731751

Rothschild, Chloe (2020) 'Feeling comfortable and understood by my medical community.' Geek Book Clubs, Autism Storytelling, February 17. Available at: https://geekclubbooks.com/2020/02/feeling-comfortable-and-understood-by-medical-community

Salseda, Lindsay M., Dennis R. Dixon, Tracy Fass, Deborah Miora, and Robert A. Leark (2011) 'An evaluation of *Miranda* rights and interrogation in autism spectrum disorders.' *Research in Autism Spectrum Disorders 5*, 1, 79–85. Available at: www.sciencedirect.com/science/article/abs/pii/S1750946710001017?via%3Dihub

Shapiro, Joseph (2018) 'The sexual assault epidemic no one talks about.' *NPR*, January 8. Available at: www.npr.org/2018/01/08/570224090/the-sexual-assault-epidemic-no-one-talks-about

Soares, Neelkamal, Kathryn E. White, Robert T. Christensen, Audrey Christiansen, and Roger Apple (2019) 'Collaborating with families and law enforcement agencies to improve outcomes for individuals with autism spectrum disorder.' *Journal of Developmental & Behavioral Pediatrics 40*, 9, 659–68. Available at: https://journals.lww.com/jrnldbp/Abstract/2019/12000/Collaborating_with_Families_and_Law_Enforcement.1.aspx

Szalavitz, Maia (2017) 'The hidden link between autism and addiction.' *The Atlantic*, March 2. Available at: www.theatlantic.com/health/archive/2017/03/autism-and-addiction/518289

The Minnesota Governor's Council on Developmental Disabilities (2021) 'The Self-Advocacy Movement 1980–.' Available at: https://mn.gov/mnddc/parallels/seven/7a/1.html

UK Safer Internet Centre (2018) *Digital friendships: The role of technology in young people's relationships.* Available at: www.saferinternet.org.uk/digital-friendships

US EEOC (United States Equal Employment Opportunity Commission) (no date) 'Disability discrimination.' Available at: www.eeoc.gov/disability-discrimination

Whetzel, Melanie (2010) 'Interviewing tips for applicants with autism spectrum disorders (ASD).' *Consultants' Corner 10*, 1, JAN (Job Accommodation Network). Available at: https://askjan.org/publications/consultants-corner/vol10iss01.cfm?cssearch=2908502_1

Online Resources

Apartment Therapy, a home and decor site: www.apartment-therapy.com

ASAN (Autistic Self Advocacy Network) provides information about autism, disability rights, and systems change to the public through a number of different educational, cultural, and advocacy-related projects: https://autisticadvocacy.org

Autism Personal Coach provides autistic adults and teens the support to live self-sufficient and purpose-driven lives through private coaching and community events: https://autism personalcoach.com

AWN (Autistic Women & Nonbinary Network) offers community, support, and resources for autistic women, girls, transfeminine and transmasculine nonbinary people, trans people of all genders, Two Spirit people, and all others of marginalized genders: https://awnnetwork.org

BetterHelp aims to make professional counseling accessible, affordable, and convenient: www.betterhelp.com

JAN (Job Accommodation Network), a project funded by the US Department of Labor, does an excellent job outlining accommodations for autistic workers: https://askjan.org/disabilities/Autism-Spectrum.cfm

KultureCity, a leading nonprofit on sensory accessibility and acceptance for those with invisible disabilities: www.kulturecity.org

National Disability Rights Network works in Washington, DC on behalf of the Protection and Advocacy Systems (P&As) and Client Assistance Programs (CAPs), the US's largest providers of legal advocacy services for people with disabilities: http://ndrn.org

People First is an organization run by and for people with learning difficulties: https://peoplefirstltd.com

SABE (Self Advocates Becoming Empowered) has a mission to ensure that people with disabilities are treated as equals and that they are given the same decisions, choices, rights, responsibilities, and chances to speak up to empower themselves, as well as opportunities to make new friends and to learn from their mistakes: www.sabeusa.org

Talkspace offers comprehensive online mental health treatment options: www.talkspace.com

Wrong Planet provides a discussion forum where members communicate with each other, an article section with exclusive articles and how-to guides, a blogging feature, and more: https://wrongplanet.net

Index

A Freshman Survival Guide for College Students with Autism Spectrum Disorders
The Stuff Nobody Tells You About!
Haley Moss

£14.99 | $19.95 | PB | 160PP |
ISBN 978 1 84905 984 8 |
eISBN 978 0 85700 922 7

How do you know which college is right for you? What happens if you don't get on with your roommate? And what on earth is the Greek system all about? As a university student with High-Functioning Autism, Haley Moss offers essential tips and advice in this insider's guide to surviving the Freshman year of college.

Chatty, honest and full of really useful information, Haley's first-hand account of the college experience covers everything students with Autism Spectrum Disorders need to know. She talks through getting ready for college, dorm life and living away from parents, what to expect from classes, professors and exams, and how to cope in new social situations and make friends.

This book is a must-read for all students on the autism spectrum who are about to begin their first year of college, parents and teachers who are helping them prepare, and college faculty and staff.